Acclaim for *Noı*

"Great stuff!! Took me right back to my childhood, from the five-finger discount to the blood and guts fun!"

Rob Gibson, Wheat Ridge, CO

"It draws me in. It just has that fidgety boy energy, and I can so feel the emotion of the experience as I read!"

Cheryl Smith, Santa Rosa, CA

"I laughed out loud for most every chapter. I was reading it at work and everyone asked me what was so funny."

Amy Ferreira, Austin, TX

"A very whimsical romp. Great insight into the very core of childhood and adolescence. Tender and sweet when it needs to be. Cute to laugh-out-loud funny when the circumstances arise."

David Gibbs, Unionville, CT

"I have to say that this was a very easy, fun read. It definitely took me back to my mischievous and awkward younger days."

Cassie Ward, Denver, CO

"I really enjoyed reading this!"

Joslynn Badders, Centennial, CO

"At first I thought it was a book that I could read one story and put down, but as I got farther into it, I found that I needed the next piece."

Felipe Botero, Flemington, NJ

"At times, I found myself laughing out loud!"

Kylie Wilson, Des Moines, IA

Nowhere Near Manhood

Michael Mecherikoff

Karen,

I'm so glad to have met you! I look forward to more conversations over bagels and coffee.

M. Mecherikoff

BLB Bridge Light Books
Denver • Colorado

Copyright 2009 by Michael Mecherikoff

ATTENTION MAGAZINES, E-ZINES, NEWSPAPERS, AND OTHER PERIODICALS: Individual stories within *Nowhere Near Manhood* are available for excerpt and publication. For information, please contact Bridge Light Books PO Box 351462, Westminster, CO 80035-1462, USA; Email: Michael@BridgeLightBooks.com.

All rights reserved. No part of this publication may be reproduced, distributed, or transmitted in any form or by any means, or stored in a database or retrieval system, without the prior written permission of the author, except by a reviewer who may quote brief passages in a review.

Cover photo and design by Chandra Mecherikoff
Cover and book layout by Christine Bennett
Author photo by Christine Bennett

The Bridge Light Books name and logo are trademarks of
Bridge Light Books, Inc.
PO Box 351462
Westminster, CO 80035-1462
www.BridgeLightBooks.com

Author's note: The events and characters described in these stories are true, to the best of the author's recollection. Most of the names have been changed to protect privacy, but some people were bound to be found out, anyway.

ISBN: 978-0-557-08221-6
Library of Congress Control Number: 2009907013

**Get your copy of *Nowhere Near Manhood!*
www.NowhereNearManhood.com**

Printed in the United States of America

For my family.

Contents

Introduction	1
Mind in the Gutter	5
Mr. Universe	13
Kitchen Pirates	17
Thou Shalt Not Steal	25
Mack	35
Pornucopia	53
A Martyr for Coolness	65
What Would MacGuyver Do?	77
The Marlboro Men	85
Brotherly Love	89
Big Man on Campus	95
TP	103
Sisterly Influence	115
Black...with Red Trim	123

Show-Off	129
Joyride	143
In with the Out Crowd	149
Undies on Stage	153
Halloweenie	163
Accidents & Opportunities	169
K-i-s-s-i-n-g	175
Underage	181
Acknowledgments	193

Introduction

That I'm alive is a fluke. At birth I tried to strangle myself with my own umbilical cord, which should have triggered my parents to dress me in full body armor and keep me on a short leash. Instead, I spent much of my childhood maiming myself. But along with laughing at bodily noises, frequent injury is just part of being a boy.

That boys survive to become men at all is proof that luck exists. We're naturally attracted to certain things; those things are either sharp, in pieces, or on fire—or they're about to be. As I shared the following memories with now-adult male friends, they reminisced about their own thoughtless, dangerous, painful, illegal, meaningless, and immature adventures. "I went through that phase," one regaled, "where we tried building all kinds of random explosive devices out of hairspray and other assorted household chemicals." I'm tellin' ya, it's luck.

If you're the mother of a young boy or two, these stories may help you to accept that the mind-boggling stunts your boys perform are, believe it or not, normal. And if you're an expectant mother whose friends and relatives are buying pastel-blue blankets and miniature pro-sports uniforms for that little guy on the way, *Nowhere Near Manhood* may shed some light on what you can expect after the stork wishes you good luck and flies away, snickering.

For you men out there, enjoy your walk down Memory Lane.

Michael Mecherikoff
June 23, 2008

Mind in the Gutter

Homer Simpson put it best: "Kids are so stupid."

From an adult perspective, it's amazing to consider the mindless activities children engage in, totally absent the concerns we pick up as we get older. Equally amazing is that natural selection hasn't claimed more of the little demons.

Kids dash into busy streets for nothing more valuable than a ball. They accept life-threatening dares long before they accept the label "chicken." They eat food—and things not intended to be food—from the floor, from the sidewalk, from the sandbox. They pick their noses, pick at scabs, pick at gum under restaurant tables. They lie, they cheat, they steal. And best of all, they try to wriggle their way out of myriad illogical and often unbelievable behaviors with two big eyes and two little words: I dunno.

My brother Cameron and I, at four and six, employed this explanation the night the police brought us home.

Camarillo is not a large city. In fact, unless you know someone living near Los Angeles, you've probably never heard of it. Supermarkets, schools, the usual fast food. It's an average bedroom community, once known to locals for its mental hospital and now famous throughout Los Angeles and surrounding counties for its outlet mall.

In the early- to mid-1980s, our neighborhood in Camarillo was a Norman Rockwell painting: kids yelling and playing hide-n-seek, a friendly dog and its owner playing tug-of-war with a knotted sock, neighbors watering their lawns while gossiping about other neighbors. In the evening, mothers' voices blared over the three-bedroom houses like air-raid sirens, warning their children to duck and cover or to come home for dinner. Either way, Cameron and I were usually inside within a few minutes.

Our neighborhood on this arid afternoon, however, was sunny and void of life, like a Rockwell painting from which the people had been abducted, leaving Cameron and me without entertainment. But give a boy almost any object, and if his mind is in the right place, his imagination runs with it. Would two dead branches suffice? Absolutely.

Adventuresome lads at six and four, we sought treasure and trouble and usually found both; our standards for treasure were pretty low. Mimicking me, Cameron snapped the twigs and leaves from his small branch, and like Frosty the Snowman our diviners suddenly came to life, pointed themselves toward the nearest water, and began leading us like tour guides along the water's course; i.e., the gutter.

At the corner of Blue Oak Street, the sidewalk bent left onto Baywood Avenue, lined the cul-de-sac of homes and yards and abandoned bicycles, and pointed us back to Blue Oak. We followed our wooden adventure guides south, away from home, toward Lantana Street, where they crossed the road, took a right, and led onward past a series of quaint, single-story houses and mailboxes on posts.

With the glee of tourists we followed our leaders across Coe Street and Red Oak Place, past Pinehurst Place and Woodgate Court, taking in the sights and sounds of suburb life. The smell of rotting avocados filled the air, prompting our guides to hasten the pace. When the occasional Firebird or Beatle got in the way, they led us onto the curb, then back into the gutter. And all the while they kept our destination a secret.

The conversations Cameron and I shared as children, about swear words and BMX bikes and human anatomy, lasted only minutes. So I can't imagine what would have occupied our young minds for this two-hour tour if boys couldn't be entertained by things as trivial as sticks in a gutter. Like I said, our standards: low.

As we crossed Ponderosa Drive and entered Camarillo's modest town center, our eyes, having been on the gutter, took in the change in scenery. Far behind us were the yards and driveways of the neighborhood, and around us stood small office buildings and a strip mall. Cars slowed along the road, their drivers bearing questioning looks. Our wooden guides, however, ignored the glares from those not in their two-person tour group and merrily continued.

"Hey, guys. What ya doin'?"

We froze. A rust-colored van had crept up behind us, and now the driver leaned his head of stringy hair out the window.

Even when the tone of an adult's voice is pleasant, four- and six-year-old kids can sense when they're in trouble. And although the young mind doesn't yet know the phrase that captures the frightful adrenaline rush of being caught, the young body feels it anyway: *Oh, shit.*

What were we doing?

"I dunno," we answered.

He waved a car around his van. "Where are your parents?"

"At home," I said. *Duh, where else would they be?*

And with those two words reality caught up to us. The sun was now slipping behind wispy clouds, our sneakers were drenched, and brown gutter water saturated the hems of our corduroys. Soon, hunger would awake within us and start panging for attention.

"You guys be careful, all right?"

"We will," we called.

As the man pulled away, he began talking into the handset of a CB radio, but that didn't stop us. Having highlighted the Laundromat, the liquor store, and the other shops in the plaza, our branch guides turned us around and started toward home.

Within minutes a police car braked at the curb. *Oh shit, oh shit, oh shit.* An officer approached, his eyes behind aviator glasses, and in a baritone voice he asked the same questions that the man in the van had asked. Looking at myself in his mirrored lenses, I repeated the same unconvincing answers, and he promptly loaded us into the back of his squad car. He shoved the door closed as if slamming a jail cell. Our tour guides reverted to simple sticks and lay in the gutter. Fat lot of help they were.

I had never been in a police car before, and I took a moment to look around. A net of solid, black metal extended from floor to ceiling, and windows walled us in. The doors were missing the knobs to lock or unlock them, and no window cranks were there to give the slightest notion of escape.

"How do you roll the windows down?" I asked.

The officer eyed the rearview mirror over his shades like Clint Eastwood as though I were about to make his day. "You don't," he said, and after requesting we put on seatbelts, he was sure to mention the burglars, gang members, and other criminals who usually occupied his back seat.

Cameron and I exchanged a glance. We had no idea what juvenile hall actually looked like, but older boys in the neighborhood had made us well aware of its existence.

"Um," I said just above a whisper. "Can you tell us where we're going?"

The officer waited several seconds before responding, eyes never leaving the road. "You are going home."

Phew!

By now, of course, neighbors had returned from work and were picking up toys from their lawns. I imagine the scene from their perspective: two bright blond bowl cuts and eyes barely high enough to see out the window riding through the neighborhood in the back of a cop car. *Aren't those the scalps of the Mecherikoff boys?*

We pulled to the curb on Blue Oak Street, and as I reached for the door handle, I learned firsthand about child-proof doors and claustrophobia. The officer opened my door from the outside, and Cameron slid over the seat, as our parents jogged across the blacktop driveway.

Mom took us in her arms. Dad did not.

"I've been driving around, searching for you for an hour! Mom's been calling all your friends, the hospitals," he gestured to the officer, "the police station. We were worried sick! What were you *thinking?* Where have you *been?*"

I looked up, and with two big eyes I provided a child's universal explanation: "I dunno."

Mr. Universe

There's a period in life that we call adulthood, which seems to begin the moment we start wishing we were younger. And there's another period before adulthood that we call childhood when, ironically, all we want to be is older, to do the mature things that grown-ups do, like drive and go to work and watch movies with nudity.

For many boys, part of becoming a man is the desire to grow bigger and stronger physically. This want is cultivated over time as boys learn a man's fundamental purposes in life: to lift heavy stuff, open pickle jars, and at least appear that they can beat up other boys' dads.

Yet in spite of Cameron's and my natural longing to be men, asking our parents for weightlifting equipment was like asking for cars and jobs and permission to see behind the red curtain at the video store. "You're eight and six, you don't need barbells. Now drink your milk."

Freddie Fernandez lived half a block away on Beechwood Street. He was several inches taller than Cameron or I, and several years older, too. We didn't often go to his house, and looking back I'm surprised we were hanging out with him at all. Four or five years is a world of difference between six, eight, and somewhere near thirteen. In fact, why the hell was *he* hanging out with *us*?

And then I saw it, the barbell on the floor against the wall of his bedroom. I had no idea how much it weighed, and yet it called to me. While Freddie was attending to his new ghetto blaster's detachable speakers, I began to lift. It didn't seem so heavy, until I tried getting it past my waist. Like most eight-year-old boys, I just didn't have that much in the way of shoulders.

"Cam, push from underneath while I lift."

Cameron did as told, and the barbell rose. "You got it?"

"Yeah," I grunted. "Keep going."

Before I knew it, the barbell was over my head. For a moment I stood there like a trophy with dozens of pounds above me. Then I learned the meaning of the phrase "top heavy."

If you've ever watched Olympic weightlifting, you may have noticed a few things about the athletes. One, they're kinda big. Two, when they have a gazillion pounds above their heads, they tend to position their feet correctly to support such weight. And three, they don't just stand there like they're posing for *Beefcake* magazine while holding eight times their own body weight above their heads. Had I watched Olympic weightlifting, I might have learned these few valuable lessons. What I learned at Freddie's house, however, was the cry of a man in trouble, which is grunted very quickly as a single word: "Idonthaveit!"

It happened in slow motion, my scrawny frame tipping backward while Cameron and Freddie raced to catch the weight: *"Nooooooooooo!"* The barbell boomed against the carpet, and aftershocks rippled throughout the house. I lay on my back, stunned.

"Just don't cry," Freddie said, as I began to cry. "No, *don't* cry."

A moment later, Freddie's mother appeared at the door. "What was...?"

I immediately sucked up my tears and sat up.

"Freddie, how many times have I told you—"

"He's okay, Mom. He just tried lifting too much."

"I'm okay," I said, and sniffled. I came to a wobbly stand and forced myself not to touch the throbbing at the back of my head.

"Are you sure?"

"Yeah."

"Yeah, he's okay," Cameron assured, and put a hand on my back as if feeling for soft spots.

Before Freddie's mother could say, "Why don't you boys head home while I take a belt to my son's..." we were already on our way.

Kitchen Pirates

Her skin pales and nausea issues from her core when our sister Chandra recalls babysitting Cameron and me. We were totally disobedient, somewhat abusive, occasionally violent, and always uncontrollable.

With our father at work and our mother at the YMCA early one summer morning, Chandra took the opportunity to sleep. Cameron and I were instructed to watch television and *behave*, to wake Chandra only in the event of an emergency. What could possibly go wrong if we were sitting quietly, watching the *Smurfs?*

It began with a commercial break and a wooden spoon.

"En guard!" I blurted, and slapped Cameron on the rear with the flat of the spoon while he poured

Honey Nut Cheerios into a bowl. He yelped, and tiny Os spewed onto the counter.

The drawer of kitchen implements remained open, and he, too, opted for a wooden spoon. *Clack, clack, clack! Clack, clack, clack!* The sword-like motions were repeated and quickly became boring. *Clack. Clack. Clack.* We had learned from Bugs Bunny cartoons that this was not how sword fighting was supposed to go. Opponents were supposed to flip backwards off of barrels while leaping over each others' swords and swing from thick ropes and elaborate chandeliers and ships' sails. And the muted sound of two wooden spoons connecting wasn't even close to the *CHING!* of two swords.

In the drawer lay a metal serving spoon with a broken, plastic handle.

"*Touché!*" I exclaimed, and withdrew the spoon from the drawer like a sword from a scabbard.

The dull *clunk* of Cameron's wooden spoon and the dents forming in its handle quickly proved its inferiority. He stopped and exchanged the spoon for an egg beater, sending us into a fit of hysterics while we continued our clash.

Click, click, click! Click, click, click!

He ducked and jabbed me in the knee. "*Touché*, yourself, buttface."

Laughter roared. Then, "Oh, yeah?" I countered, and replaced the metal spoon with a carving knife.

Cameron observed the egg beater in his hand. It may have defended him, but his ego would surely suffer heavy blows. Buried beneath a variety of other tools and attachments was a breadknife whose length was its notable advantage.

Ching, ching, ching! Ching, ching, ching! Our backward flips were no more than small backward steps, and no elaborate chandelier hung from the kitchen ceiling, so the sound of two long knives making contact was as close to a cartoon swordfight as we were going to get.

Ching, ching, ching. Ching, ching, OW, SHIT!

I dropped my knife onto the counter and immediately saw blood, which triggered the stinging that sent my hand into a flailing motion. Drops of blood flew everywhere.

"I'm sorry! I'm sorry! Are you okay?" Before attending to me, Cameron scrambled to bury the breadknife in the drawer, as if he'd never seen it.

"Do I look okay?! Get me a paper towel. Run some water on it. *Cold* water."

He obeyed immediately, and I wrapped my thumb inside the cool paper towel, holding it over the sink.

The bleeding just wouldn't stop. But since Cameron had complied instantly with my previous order, I decided to take advantage of my power position.

"Go get Chandra!" I barked.

Again he snapped to obedience, and Chandra appeared in the kitchen in pajamas.

If she had seen how small the cut really was, she may have put a Band-Aid on it, sent us to our rooms, and gone back to bed. And for once we might have obeyed. Instead, she saw the dampened paper towel. Blood had soaked into it and spread by the water, making it appear as though my thumb were lying in the kitchen sink. She rolled her eyes, told me to put a dry paper towel on it, and called our mother at the YMCA.

Mom in her sweat pants and I in my tractor-print jammies arrived at the ER, signed in, and sat in the waiting room for the inevitable mispronunciation of my name.
"Michael Muuuh...." We looked up at the nurse. "C'mon back. How do you say your last name?"
"Meh-share-i-cough," Mom explained.
The nurse nodded, looking confused, and led us to a small room. The doctor would be with us soon.
Wax paper crackled as Mom set me on the examination table. In addition to sweat clothes, a salty line below her plastic-frame trifocals and her dark, tossed curls evidenced the aerobics class she left in order to attend to me. She chose an issue of *Family Circle* from a rack on the wall and inquired about my thumb. It was throbbing again, I told her. She nodded, expecting nothing less, and sat with the magazine.
If there's anything more painful to a child than bleeding, it's boredom. I sat there, thumb beating like a heart,

eying jars of tongue depressors and cotton balls, which, if I'd had access to them, would have become a medieval catapult and boulders.

When the doctor arrived, he greeted us and removed the paper towel to see the tip of my thumb hanging like a tiny flag.

"How'd you do this?"

Mom answered for me. "He and his brother thought it'd be a good idea to sword fight with kitchen knives."

The doctor nodded. He'd seen worse, probably that morning.

"We started with wooden spoons," I sheepishly explained.

"Probably should've stuck with 'em," he responded, and pulled latex gloves over his hands. "All right, Michael, I'll need you to be really brave." Translation: This is gonna hurt like hell.

He pinched the tiny flap of skin with a pair of tweezers.

"Ready? One. Two—" *Rip!*

What about three?! I thought, and in that same instant a flood of searing hot pain rushed through me and nearly escaped in a highly concentrated and very girlish scream. The doctor handed me a fold of gauze from a jar.

"All right. You okay?"

For some reason I nodded.

"Good. Now we need to disinfect it."

He led us to another room and placed a small container on the examination table, then filled it with a red liquid.

"What's that?" I asked.

"This? It's called a bedpan."

"No, I mean, is that blood you're pouring into it?"

"No," he laughed, "that's Betadine."

If this doctor had had unruly boys of his own, they weren't unruly for long. He seemed to know a variety of tactics to teach children the repercussions of misbehavior.

He gently pinched my thumb and lowered it into the bedpan, then squeezed. For a second, a cool sensation covered my fingers. Then fire raced up my arm and scorched my very soul.

"Ow, it hurts, it's burning!"

The doctor held my quivering thumb as though he were drowning it. "It'll be gone in a moment," he uttered, possibly referring to the thumb itself, and slowly removed his hand from mine. "Just hold still."

My lip quivered, my eyes about to let loose. "How long do I have to keep my hand here?"

"Ten minutes," he said. "I'll be back then."

Ten minutes?! That's an *eternity* when you're six, even when your finger's not disintegrating in acid! As he closed the door behind him, I turned to my mom for comfort.

"Well that's what you get for playing with knives."

The doctor returned what seemed like six hours later, and my hand was stained red. He produced a wood rasp cleverly disguised as a brush and scrubbed the open wound in a nearby sink. My clenched teeth nearly cracked. Finally, after rinsing my hand, he led us back to the first room.

With an amazing little gadget as simple looking as an oversized thimble, he wrapped a gauze bandage around the length of my thumb, then taped the end in place. The throbbing seemed softened by the cotton wrapping.

"Just keep it clean and dry. And try to avoid knives."

"Thank you," Mom said, as the doctor turned and left the room. "You hear that?"

I smirked. "Yes."

I don't remember my exact explanation to the other neighborhood boys, but I imagine it went something like this:

"Man, what happened to your thumb?"

"Shark attack."

Thou Shalt Not Steal

We began with Brach's candies, the little, gummy kind that ten out of ten dentists will tell you you'll go to hell just for thinking about. Chocolate and caramel wrapped in shiny plastic like little nuggets of gold. Oh, those things were great! The way they clung to your teeth as you chewed them, leaving flavor in your mouth long after you'd swallowed the little wad of sugar. Hours later you'd find pieces that had escaped into that space between your gum and lip, and you'd be hit with another burst of sweet, sweet flavor! So tasty and yet so small. And the best part, they were free.

Some smart marketing peon quickly became a marketing exec when he designed a candy rack that stood at children's eye level. Several plastic bins, each filled with three gallons of these bite-size wonders, stood near the end of the candy aisle at the local Safeway grocery store. To get there from our house on Blue Oak Street was a 20-minute bike ride, which was nothing when we were boys, even in the summer sun. We'd lean our bikes against the wall outside the store and then wander the various departments, looking inconspicuous—right there along with all the other six- and eight-year-old boys spending their summer days eyeing deli meat and sampling bites of microwave pizza on toothpicks. After several minutes of meandering, we'd just, ya know, happen into the candy aisle.

It was a quick job, no more than a few pieces in each pocket, and we were out the door and on our getaway bikes.

"What happens if someone ever stops us on the way out?" Cameron asked, unwrapping a candy, hands free of the handlebars.

I thought for a moment. "We'll just tell them we didn't find what we were looking for."

He squeezed his reply over the lump of caramel in his mouth: "O-kuh."

We had our routine down. It was easy and exciting: a quick stroll around the store, pocket a few candies, and ride away. This free-stuff thing was great!

Late one morning, while biking through the supermarket's parking lot, Cameron noticed something mysterious on the ground near a massive garbage container beside the store. It shimmered in the sun, seeming to wink as we rode closer. A sausage!

It was mighty: eight inches long and four in circumference. Wrapped in plastic, it looked like all the other sausages on the store shelves. So why had someone tried to throw this one away? We were aware of the natural processes of decomposition and rotting (our teeth, obviously, were beyond our concern), but this specimen was wrapped in plastic and appeared—by boys' standards, anyway—perfectly suitable for consumption.

Just to be safe, I carried the sausage to a neighbor's house where a Doberman pinscher tore across the yard and chomped at the fence boards each time we rode by. With a pocket knife I kept hidden from my parents I cut open the wrapper and tossed the slimy log of processed meat over the fence. Within the five seconds I spent wiping grease onto the legs of my shorts, the beast bit the dirt-covered sausage in half, wolfed down both pieces, and flew back to the fence, ready to take the same action on Cameron and me.

"WHY'D YOU DO THAT?!" Cameron shouted over the barking.

"DUDE," I shouted back. "YOU CAN'T JUST EAT A SAUSAGE YOU FOUND IN A PARKING LOT! YOU HAVE TO TEST IT FIRST!"

"BUT YOU THREW THE *WHOLE THING* IN THERE!"

"I KNOW!" I yelled back, and condescendingly rubbed Cameron's newly shaved head. "THERE'LL BE MORE!"

He reached for my head to return the insult, but I ducked and rode away.

The next morning we woke knowing where we'd be going. On the way to Safeway, we slowed on the street near the Doberman, which flew across the yard and tore at the fence. "SEE?!" I shouted to Cameron over the rabid beast. "IT'S STILL ALIVE!" And on we rode.

Bypassing the storefront altogether, we hid our bikes behind Safeway's giant Dumpster and poked our blond heads from behind it. The coast was clear. We climbed in.

By the time we pulled ourselves out of the garbage bin and rode away, we had eaten our fill of sausage. Little did we think that it probably had been there since the day before—at *least*—or that we had just eaten lunch inside a massive garbage container. And while we were thoughtful enough to shove a couple extra sausages into our pockets for the neighbor's Doberman, we had not yet owned a dog and therefore had no concept of the digestive effects that eating two logs of spicy sausage might have on it and, ultimately, on its owners.

A few times a week we climbed into the Dumpster, but often the bounty was more disappointing than worthwhile. Let's be realistic, we were boys and had no qualms about doing things that 20 years later we'd file under D for Disgusting, but how many times were we gonna jump into a giant trash bin for expired food? Back into the store we went.

Having forgotten about our old routine, we headed directly to the candy aisle. And something in that shift sealed our fate. I was familiarizing myself with the current array of Brach's candies when:

"Pst! *Pssssssst!* What about this?" Cameron asked, holding a Hershey bar. It was obvious: the sausage had corrupted him.

"No, it's too big."

"No, it's not," he argued. "Just try." He crammed it into my pocket.

"No, dude, it's too *big*." Did he not realize that you can take a giant sausage out of a garbage bin without hiding it because...well, it's garbage and no one cares? I pulled the chocolate out of my pocket and reached to return it to the shelf.

"Oh, c'mon," Cameron said. "Chicken."

Well that shut me up. I looked around, and seeing no one else in the aisle, I tried to jam the six-inch bar into my four-inch pocket.

"Okay, c'mon." I kept my right arm at my side, palm sweating against the exposed two inches.

From the store's automatic door the afternoon sunshine looked warm and inviting...

"Hi," a man said.

...And it'd be a while before we saw it again.

He wore a vest, a blue tie around the neck of a white collared shirt, and a pair of ironed khakis. "Where ya going?"

Oh, shit. We froze, slack-jawed and stunned. Fortunately, we had planned for this moment.

"Home," I said.

"We didn't find what we were looking for," Cameron added, and smiled at me.

"Oh? What were you looking for?"

Our plan hadn't taken us that far, and my lying skills were about as good as my method for testing sausage for edibility.

Fortunately, a boy always has two answers in his holster, ready to fire at any time: *I dunno*, and, "Nothing."

The store manager crossed his arms. "You came into Safeway looking for…'nothing'?"

I could've told him anything, that we were just using the bathroom or that I realized I had forgotten my wallet in my other pants. But I couldn't go back on my answer now. I nodded.

"Mm-hm. You know, shoplifting is a crime."

We looked up at him, two bristle-headed boys with completely empty expressions.

"Stealing," he clarified. He held out his hand and motioned toward my pocket. I laid the candy bar on his palm. "Come with me, boys."

We were so close to the front door, we should have just

run as the manager turned his back. But when a boy is in trouble, when his body is wrapped in that *oh shit* sensation, his mind is nowhere to be found. *Screw this, I'm outta here*, it tells him, leaving behind the shell of a dumbfounded kid.

The manager led us to a customer service desk at the front of the store and took out a pen.

"What's your phone number?"

He wrote it down as I told him. I could sense Cameron's eyes on me and I turned.

You moron, his face expressed.

This is your fault, buttface, my eyes replied before turning back to the manager.

"Please don't call our parents," I said. "Please?" And in a moment of brilliance: "They're not even home right now."

"Oh, where are they?" He finished dialing and held the ringing phone to his ear.

"Our dad's at work and our mom's at the YMCA."

In spite of my groveling he let the phone ring, and when no one answered he hung up. Thank God Chandra liked to sleep late.

"I'm going to hang on to this," he said, pinching the register slip with our phone number on it. "I don't ever want to see you boys in this store again."

"Okay."

"Okay."

Near the edge of the parking lot, our bikes skidded to a stop. Our mother's station wagon passed on the opposite side of the street. *She knows. But how? We just talked to the manager.* It didn't matter. We were dead meat.

"Ya know," Cameron said, "you could've given him a fake number."

Damn! I wished I had thought of that.

We watched Mom's station wagon pass. No doubt it was hers—Ford LTD with sun-bleached wood paneling—and yet it didn't slow. She didn't even notice us.

As we rode toward home, we passed the Doberman, sorry that we'd never have another sausage for it. Then Cameron stopped.

"WAIT!" he called over the dog's explosive barking. "WE CAN'T GO HOME YET!"

"WHY NOT?!"

"BECAUSE AS SOON AS MOM AND DAD FIND OUT, WE'LL BE IN TROUBLE! WHAT IF MOM ALREADY KNOWS?!"

"BUT SHE'S NOT THERE!" I said. "HOW WOULD SHE KNOW?!"

"CHANDRA'S THERE!"

I nodded. "YOU'RE RIGHT!" Why waste the remainder of a perfectly sunny summer day in trouble and restricted to our rooms?

We turned around, rode in the opposite direction of

home, and eventually arrived at what appeared to be an abandoned barn, where our next adventure lay wagging its matted tail in the dirt.

Mack

When Chandra was fourteen, Cameron and I were eight and six, and what teenage girl wants anything to do with her stupid kid brothers? We were hell to babysit, fighting with each other, fighting with her, cutting off fingertips, or at the very least ignoring her every request. We were young and full of energy. We needed to *live*, damn it, to get on our bikes and *ride*! And she gladly took every opportunity to boot us out of the house, wherever we might end up, ditch or otherwise.

Having been banned from Safeway, we rode past Camarillo's YMCA—careful to distance ourselves from Mom's vacant station wagon in the Y's parking lot—to what appeared to be a derelict farm just beyond the border of normal civilization. The asphalt stopped, and a dirt road began, leading past a small, wooden tool shed to a round-roof, aluminum barn. The surrounding fields were bright tan like sun-bleached crops, and not a machine, a pitchfork, nor was even a spade in sight. Just a dog.

It was a flop-eared German shepherd mix, bound with twine to the door handle of the barn. We avoided it at first and began our adventuring at the small tool shed. But if you're a curious boy or his brother—and we were both—you can avoid a friendly-looking dog and the barn behind it only for so long.

It did little as we approached, only blinked its eyes to bat away flies. As we neared and spoke in that silly voice people reserve for babies and dogs, it raised its head.

"Hold on," I said. "He's not wagging his tail anymore."

We lowered and stretched our hands to its nose, then leaned away as it stood, shook a cloud of dirt from its coat, and took three small steps before coming to the end of its string.

"Good boy," I said slowly, and Cameron repeated. We stroked the dog with the soft touches of children.

It had no tags, and the farm appeared as populous as a distant planet. The only sign of human interaction this animal had, other than that it wasn't starving, was the twine collar deeply recessed into the skin of its neck. The dog obviously was there to prevent potential thieves from entering the barn, but when we opened the adjacent barn door, there was nothing inside that appeared to be worth protecting, or from our youthful perspective even worth playing with. We closed the door and returned to the shed and the few sharp, rusty tools within.

The dog was there the next day, same place, same collar, and not a soul around. We were no experts on animal cruelty—this was the summer we used a neighbor's Doberman to test the expiration date of sausage—but a twine collar seemed inhumane.

We returned several days in a row, to the point where the dog now stood and wagged its tail each time we arrived. We parked our bikes near it and gave it some affection. It was getting food and water from somewhere, but as much exercise as a calf soon to be veal. After a couple of weeks of daily visits, I made up my mind and applied my pocket knife to the twine knotted around the door handle.

"What are you doing?" Cameron asked, and looked around.

"What's it look like I'm doing?"

"You can't do that. What if he runs away?"

"He's not gonna run away. He likes us."

"Well, what are you gonna do with him?"

"Take him home, *duuuh*."

I tied a loop at the end of the string, hooked it to a grip on my handlebars, and started pedaling. And immediately I realized that the dog now had control of my bike. Loop in my right hand, a handgrip in the left, we set off for home.

∙∙∙

"What in the—"

"Can we keep him, Mom, please?!"

"Whose dog is that? Yick, it's filthy!" She turned her head in disgust, apparently able to smell something we boys were impervious to.

"We found him at this barn and he was tied up and all by himself!"

Taking shallow breaths, Mom looked over the dog and traced its neck with a hovering fingertip.

"Poor thing," she said, but clearly didn't want to touch it. "A barn?"

Though farming plots lay on the far outskirts of Camarillo, they were nowhere near our house, so saying that the mongrel had been tied up at a barn was as believable as saying it had been tied up in Kansas. Mom's face twisted into two questions: *Where is there a barn around here?* and, *What trouble were you two getting into at a barn?* But the twine corroborated our story, and she asked to see the place. Cameron and I coaxed the dog into the family station wagon.

And sure enough, there was the barn.

"Can we keep him, Mom?" I asked, and produced my own set of puppy-dog eyes. "Pleeease?"

Cameron saw me and followed suit. "Pleeease?"

She let the dirty, hairy beast out of the back end of the station wagon. It stood beside us and shook its coat, tail up but not wagging, as though it enjoyed our attention but recognized its unhappy surroundings.

"You can't just take a dog from someone's property," she replied. "It belongs to someone."

Our puppy-dog faces became our PO'd faces.

"Oh, c'mon, don't gimme that look. How would you feel if someone just came to our house and took something of yours that's important to you?"

Little did she know that soon we would find out.

"Mom, he's not important to anyone," I pleaded.

"Except us!" Cameron inserted.

"Yeah. No one's taking care of him. We haven't seen anyone here in like two weeks."

You've been coming here for two weeks? her eyes said, and then surveyed the property for damage. "Well, *someone's* feeding it."

She was right. The dog was not fat, and even dripping wet it wouldn't have appeared skinny. I wasn't giving up.

"If someone loved him...like *we* would," I pleaded, "they wouldn't tie him up so tight and leave him here all alone."

"Yeah," Cameron agreed. "We would love him and take care of him."

We crouched on either side of the filthy animal and held it. The dog licked at our faces.

Mom huffed and closed the station wagon's back door. "We'll talk to Dad when he gets home."

The dog stood at the edge of the dirt road that led

to the barn, its tail lowering as we waved through the rear window.

"Daddy!" We hugged his waist as he lowered his briefcase to the entryway floor. We often met him at the door when he returned from work, but extra enthusiasm was needed here. At our mother's instructions we let go of him, and within ten minutes he'd changed his clothes and gathered us to the table for dinner.

"We found a dog, Dad!" Cameron said.

Dad's attention was on his meatloaf, and his reply was the typical half-question/half-statement that parents give in response to their child's minor accomplishments: "You *di-id?*"

"Yeah. At a barn."

He looked up quizzically. Mom nodded.

"And where is it now?" he asked, eying the doorways of the adjacent rooms.

"Mom took him back," I muttered, and poked at a tater tot with my fork.

"Oh. How did you come across it?"

"We were just riding our bikes by the Y and there he was, so we became his friends."

"He's *really* friendly," Cameron added.

"And you brought it here?" Dad asked me. "Were you planning on keeping it?"

"He's not an *it*, Dad, he's a *he*. And, yeah. I mean,

he's all alone out there, tied up outside like he has rabies or something." Our parents exchanged a glance. "No one's even there with him."

"Didn't bite you, did it?" Dad swallowed. "I mean, *he*."

"No!" I exclaimed at the accusation.

"Hm. Sounds like it belongs to someone." Dad cut another bite of meatloaf with the side of his fork and dipped it in ketchup. "Do you think it's—*he's*—a guard dog?"

If I had answered, I would have stepped into his trap and lost the discussion. Of course it was a guard dog, *somebody's* guard dog, regardless of how ineffective it was. But I didn't want to admit that, to myself or to anyone. Instead, I filled my mouth.

"Smaller bites, Mike," Mom said. "Just because you're upset doesn't give you the right to eat like a pig."

Cameron laughed, and I fought back a stuffed-mouth smile.

"Well, it's probably there guarding someone's property," Dad said. "This *barn* or whatever."

I couldn't argue with that. I scarfed down my meatloaf and tater tots, drank my milk, and asked to be excused.

"Not till you finish your broccoli."

•••

My father was a larger-than-average man in both height and weight, with gradually thinning and graying blond hair and light, plastic-framed glasses. He wore a tie at the office and jeans at home. His cheeks always held a jolly redness, while the crease between his eyes evidenced the academic background and ceaseless thinking that earned him his PhD. He was a recognized intellectual, a scientist, an analyst.

I try nowadays to imagine the expression on his learned face when he stepped out the front door the next morning and found a German shepherd between him and *The Daily News*. The dog had somehow tracked its way back to our house and now lay on the mat outside our front door as if to say, "Welcome *this*."

With Cameron's and my unrelenting promises to walk and feed it and our mother's added concern about its neck, we were allowed to keep the dog. We promptly named it Mack.

•••

Children are some of the best manipulators. If every salesperson had the cute, persuasive qualities of children, the occupation would rank with doctor and lawyer in terms of financial success. *Sure, Dad, we promise to walk him and feed him. Of course, Mom, we'll give him baths and brush his fur.*

We didn't intend to make suckers of our parents, it just happened that way. Truthfully, we did want to care for

Mack, but this was our first shot at being responsible for... well, anything, much less a living creature, and we needed frequent reminding. In truth, our parents took care of Mack much more than Cameron and I ever did.

Tending to the twine around its neck, Mom was the one who brought out the scissors. And when Mack wouldn't let her get within four yards of him with scissors, Mom was the hero who, after several minutes of struggle and obvious discomfort with toenail clippers, finally took Mack to the vet and later rubbed medicated ointment into his wounded skin. Our parents fed him and let him outside. They took him to get shots and to get groomed. They paid for the collar, the leash, the bowls, the food, the registration, the carpet cleaning. In my own defense, I did take him for walks. Sometimes.

Within the first few strolls through the neighborhood I became aware of Mack's protective and aggressive nature. He growled at approaching neighbors, more often at men than at women. If Mack and I neared a man walking on the sidewalk in the opposite direction, I pulled the leash tight and let the man pass unharmed, though certainly intimidated.

On one occasion while I was watching *Growing Pains*, Mack clawed and howled with unusual fervor at the sliding glass door to the backyard. As many pet owners do, I waited till a commercial and absently opened the slider. The dog flew into the back yard, snared a cat in its teeth, and shook it wildly, ignoring my commands to drop it. White, fluffy hair fell like feathers from a ripped pillow.

•••

"Mike, you promised to walk your dog," my mom reminded me from the kitchen, frustration in her voice.

I called over the TV in the den, "I will."

"It's getting late."

"I will."

"Now!"

Through the window in the den I could see that night had already fallen. Mom's command was not to imply that something might happen to a child roaming the neighborhood beneath the streetlights—a German shepherd weighing at least as much as I did squashed that notion—rather that bedtime was right around the corner. I buckled Mack's collar, clipped on his leash, and let him drag me out the front door.

We walked to the end of the block, crossed Baywood Avenue, and continued on Blue Oak Street toward Lantana. A neighbor, Mrs. Mason, approached from the opposite direction. She was a thin woman, early forties, glasses, and permed brown hair with gray woven throughout.

As she neared, I stepped into a strip of ivy that separated the sidewalk from the street. "You may want to go around us," I called to her. "My dog sometimes bites."

Mrs. Mason continued along her path without a word or really any kind of reaction at all. To my human eyes, she didn't appear particularly masculine, or in Mack's defense particularly feminine. But just like people sometimes question the gender of dogs before looking closely, I suppose dogs question the gender of some people.

As Mrs. Mason passed, Mack sprang forth and nipped her forearm. She didn't appear to be bleeding or even hurt at all, only surprised and a little frightened. She fled quickly, and I continued in the opposite direction. *Told ya.*

•••

The following morning Mom was feeling ill, so Cameron and I combed our hair and went to church with Dad. From the lobby, Dad turned left into the chapel, while Cameron and I turned right toward a hallway of classrooms where Sunday school was held. I waited for Dad to enter the chapel and Cameron to enter his classroom, and then I returned to the car, where my imagination transformed a broken window crank into a daredevil motorcycle and an empty McDonald's bag into a ramp for it. This was my routine most Sundays, and though the trash in the car often changed, the window crank was a reliable prop.

We arrived home after church, and usually I wrestled with Mack for a few minutes, washed up, and then ate lunch while watching *Fraggle Rock*. But this Sunday there was no greeting at the door.

"Mack!" I called.

Several moments quietly passed before Mom entered the living room, wiping a tissue beneath her glasses.

"Mike," she began, and sniffled. "Did Mack bite someone last night?"

"No," I said, removing my clip tie. "He jumped up and nipped at Mrs. Mason, but he didn't *bite* her."

She inhaled deeply, pulling together her strength, and looked at Dad. "The pound came by and took Mack while you guys were at church," she said to him.

"No!" I cried, and Cameron echoed. "He didn't *bite* her!"

"Well, she thinks he did."

"But he *didn't!*" I cried. "Can we go get him?"

She shook her head. "It doesn't work that way, Mike. Mack was probably abused before you guys rescued him." She sniffed again and cleared her throat. "He had a bad temper."

"So what!" I pointed to my brother. "Cameron has a bad temper sometimes and we're not taking *him* to the pound! Mack never hurt anyone! It's not fair!"

All of this was news to Dad, too, but he was quick to be rational, just in time to for Mom to tear up again.

"Mike, we can't have a mean-tempered dog in the neighborhood," Dad said.

I crossed my arms. "So what'll happen to him?"

Mom lifted her glasses to blot her eyes and cleared her throat. She breathed. "They're going to put him down."

"What's that mean?"

"It means they're going to put him to sleep," Dad explained.

"No! He's my friend!"

"I'm sorry," Mom cried, and looked to Dad.

But I understood what was happening. It was for the better. I dragged my feet to my bedroom and closed the door.

•••

Weeks, months, and seasons passed, and almost nothing changed since Mack's departure, from Cameron's and my perspectives, anyway. To Dad, who never much cared for pets in the first place, this was one less expense and inconvenience. To Mom, the carpets had fewer hairs, the clothes had fewer hairs, the cars' interiors had fewer hairs, the lint trap had fewer hairs, dinner had fewer hairs. And to both of them, the perpetual need to remind Cameron and me to do something—*anything*—to make good on our promise to care for our dog was gone. We asked for another dog, but having experienced how uninvolved Cameron and I were with Mack's maintenance, our parents had an arsenal of reasons to use against every plea we made.

We soon moved to a house on Mansfield Lane, across Las Posas Road and two miles down from our house on Blue Oak. Instead of grass in the backyard there was a pool, which provided an instant crusher to the idea of another dog. "You rarely walked Mack when we had him," Dad said. "Where do you think another dog's gonna do his business, in the pool?" That's a pretty funny image to a ten-year-old boy, but the impracticality of having a dog was clear.

•••

They say fact is stranger than fiction, and if I hadn't seen this with my own eyes, I'd have been skeptical at best.

"Miiike!" Chandra yelled from the kitchen. "Phooone!"

"Who is it?!" I yelled back from my bedroom.

The echoes in the hallway faded while she inquired.

"It's Kirk! Now put down your Barbies and come answer the phone!" She loved to torture me with that one, and each time she was certain to remove her palm from the telephone receiver and yell it so my friends could hear it loud and clear.

Kirk Spencer was the bully of our old neighborhood.

As if his threats weren't bad enough, his parents had arranged with mine to have me over for liver one night many months before. ("Do you like it?" I was eating dinner with a kid who often threatened to beat me up. And *liver* of all things. Talk about a rock and a hard place. I winced and nodded. "We have another liver lover!" the family cried in unison, as if rehearsed. How painful politeness is at times.) I answered the phone.

"Hello?"

"Hi, Mike. Um...do you really play with Barbies?"

"No," I blurted, "I don't play with Barbies. My sister's just being retarded."

Chandra snickered and continued emptying the dish washer.

"Oh. Okay. Anyway, you have to come over!"

"What? Why?" *Please don't let this be a dinner invitation.*

"Mack's back! He's on your porch at your old house!"

"Nuh-uh."

"Yeah-huh! I just saw him there!"

"Okay. I'll be there in a minute," I said, and grabbed Cameron.

I didn't talk much with Kirk after we moved to Mansfield Lane, or even before, really. A history that included the neighborhood boys making fun of him—namely Kirk the Jerk—and his threats to beat up some of those neighborhood boys—namely Cameron and me—conditioned me to leave this kid alone. And eating liver together does not best friends make.

After a quick two-mile bike ride, Cameron and I stood before our former house on Blue Oak Street beside Kirk, staring at a flop-eared German shepherd curled up on the porch. It lay there without movement like the first time we saw Mack, not even the single wag of recognition that an exhausted dog gives its owner.

"Are you sure that's Mack?" I asked Kirk.

"I dunno, it's *your* dog."

I walked a few steps closer, but remained on the street, unsure whether this was Mack returned from the pound—not to mention from the dead—or some other dog with a mirror-like resemblance. *How can it be him?* I thought. He would have to have been immune to lethal injection, escaped from the pound, and found his way back here from wherever the pound was. He *had* survived being tied to a barn door and who knows what other conditions and treatment. And he *had* tracked his way back to our house and plopped himself on our porch once before. Was this the Rasputin of dogs? No, it was simply unbelievable. This couldn't be Mack.

I could have approached, but for some reason chose not to. A couple of years before, Cameron and I approached a strange dog, befriended it, convinced our parents to adopt it, and named it Mack. Now, though, something held me back. Perhaps it was maturity, or the memory of Mack's unpredictability, or the very real possibility that this may not be Mack at all but someone else's guard dog.

"Mack!" I called, and Cameron repeated. "C'mere, boy! C'mon!"

The dog raised its head with little energy, aware that we were calling and gesturing to it. Then it lowered its head again as though it were loyal not to us or to any other person, but to the house on Blue Oak Street.

"It's not him," I said. "Let's go."

"Are you sure?" Kirk asked.

"I don't think it's him, either," Cameron agreed.

"Man, it sure looks like him." Kirk swung a leg over his bike and started off.

I took a last look as we rode away. "Yeah."

Pornucopia

Naked women have attracted me from the first time I saw one, which was, as it happened, in a bush with Cameron. I was nine.

At three or four I played *I'll Show You Mine, You Show Me Yours* with a neighbor girl in my bedroom closet, until my mother caught us giggling. And at five I played *Doctor* with a female classmate, until the teacher caught us giggling. But these were not women, and at three and five years old I was not turned on so much as I was shocked and curious. *Whoa, hold on a minute. You don't have a penis! I'm not sure what that is, but it ain't a penis!*

"C'mon," Cameron said one July afternoon. "I want to show you something."

"What is it?"

"Just c'mon."

We picked up our bikes from the driveway and were off.

"Where are we *going*?" I called, as we rode past the modest homes of our neighborhood.

"You'll see."

Ponderosa Drive splits Camarillo diagonally. We pedaled along it for several minutes before I inquired again.

"Are we close?"

"You'll see."

Soon, the Sav-On drugstore came into view, and as we rode past it:

"Cam, where are we going?"

"Shut up. We're here. Geez."

"We're not supposed to say that."

"Shut up."

"Yeah. That."

"*Shut! Up! Geez!*"

For several moments we stood on the sidewalk between the asphalt of Ponderosa Drive and a very tall bush, Cameron surveying the street in either direction for cars and passersby, while I looked at our surroundings and wondered what Cameron meant by, "We're here." When the coast cleared, he and his bike disappeared into a narrow opening in the bush, the kind of dark hole you'd expect fanged animals to leap from.

"What are you waiting for?" his forced whisper asked from the foliage.

"Is there room?" I wasn't fat; I just didn't imagine many bushes had ample space for two boys and their bicycles.

"Yes! Get in here!"

A runner neared, and I tried to appear casual, as though I hadn't just been talking to plant life. *Yep, just hangin' out, me and my bike, next to this here bush.* The moment the runner passed, I disappeared.

There was a wall behind the bush and not much more space than I'd imagined, but enough for two boys, their bikes, and three weathered issues of *Playboy*. I hadn't seen pornography before, but if any book—or pseudo-book—can be judged by its cover, this was the one. Two feminine hands with brightly painted fingernails pressed together two massive breasts; the lips remained glossy after months of weathering; and the explosion of blonde hair didn't fit within the confines of the cover. Cameron skipped the ads and the table of contents.

Wearing little to nothing, but usually in something like high heels and a necktie, women stood or lay in a variety of poses, teaching us Misguided Sex Education Lesson #1: "These are examples of women you're supposed to find attractive when you're older." Page after rain-crusty page, women arranged themselves around executive offices, beside expensive cars, and across luxurious beds, teaching us Misguided Sex Education Lesson #2:

"These are the possessions men must have in order to attract these women."

When Cameron reached the center of the magazine, he unfolded a woman who stood in a downtown office wearing nothing but heels.

"Why do you think—"

"Sh!"

"Sorry," I whispered. "Why do you think they leave their shoes on? Don't you think it'd be easier for them to take their pants off if they took their shoes off first?"

Even at seven years old Cameron was capable of showing pity and disappointment via facial expression. *Are you a moron?* his eyes asked. "You're not supposed to look at their shoes, stupid."

"Wull I, I wasn't. But I mean..."

His lips pursed. *Moron.*

Uninterested in the model's hobbies and turn-ons, Cameron thumbed through the remainder of the magazine, while I looked over his shoulder. He then took up the second issue. Same thing, just different settings, and this one featured a red-head.

Several questions I hadn't yet thought to ask were answered that day: What does a grown woman look like naked? Does a redhead have red pubic hair? Where was Cameron when he wasn't hanging out with me?

Later that summer, Cameron and I found a much more

secluded place. (*Ahem.*) Okay, *he* found the more secluded place, and by the time he brought me there, he had transported his porn stash from the bush and had added several issues of *Penthouse*. Where was he getting this stuff?

From our neighborhood this hideaway was tucked across Las Posas Road, past several acres of strawberry fields littered with shotgun shells, beyond a curiously placed jalopy, and into the hills of northern Camarillo. A lumpy, dirt trail wound along the shrub-covered hillsides and into unknown territory. As tempting as unknown territory is to young boys, our treasure lay inside a forsaken water storage tank not far from the trailhead.

The decrepit container offered very little light, but much more space and privacy than the hole in the bush by Sav-On. By its location on the hillside, it appeared to have been used long ago in connection with the strawberry farm below. Now, however, I climbed the rusty ladder, squeaked open the rusty hatch, and peered into the relative darkness to see fine sand covering the floor and a small heap of magazines seemingly dropped from above.

While many men are rumored to metamorphose into wild dogs at the sight, I've never really cared about lingerie. Underwear is underwear, as far as I'm concerned. And the expressions on the faces of the women posing in nudie magazines, eyes closed like bedroom curtains, just doesn't do it for me either. But by noon I had learned to look past the undies and "O" faces. The California sun baked the dark, rusted water tank, and sweat soaked our shirts, yet there we sat, cross-legged in the sand, flipping page after page of porn.

•••

In the years to come, this type of material happened across my path again and again, material intended for adults, but that children somehow get their hands on, like cigarette lighters, aerosol cans, or the combination of the two.

Donny Jorgen was a friend in fifth grade whose father received and apparently collected a substantial amount of such material. How Donny discovered it, or what possessed him to load several samples into his backpack and bring them to school, I never asked. He did, however, reveal this bounty to me in a fashion similar to Cameron's: "C'mon. I want to show you something."

Like a pack of Pavlovian dogs my classmates and I responded to a ringing bell, probably salivating, and filed out of the classroom for morning recess.

Bedford Elementary School shared an expansive campus with El Descanso Elementary School. The grounds for the two schools included an asphalt lot painted with various lines for hopscotch, four-square, dodgeball, basketball, and tetherball, and acres of grass, which comprised several soccer fields. Sun-faded wooden fences paralleled ancient eucalyptus trees and served to border the distant side of the schoolyard.

While teachers positioned themselves near the swings and monkey bars, Donny and I walked across the soccer fields to the base of a tree far from anyone else. We sat on the grass, and before removing his backpack, Donny surveyed the landscape—again similar to Cameron before he and his bike disappeared into the bush behind the Sav-On drugstore. At first I thought Donny had brought food, and I wondered why he had dragged me all the way out here to eat it. Instead, he produced three issues of *Playboy* and laid them on the grass.

"Whoa!" I said. "Where'd you get these?"

"My dad has a whole bunch of 'em."

"He saves 'em?" I asked, opening the first in the small stack.

Donny shrugged. "Yeah, I guess."

I imagine what we must have looked like from the teachers' perspective: two boys sitting cross-legged at the back of the field, hundreds of yards away from all the other children, glancing up with every page we turned. We could have been plotting a crime, for all they knew, a hostile takeover of the school or at least a rigging of the vote for the next class president. *Nope, Teach, just checkin' out some porn. Don't mind us.*

This became our routine for morning recess, lunch recess, and afternoon recess, five days a week. How did the teachers not question the sight of two boys wandering off to the far reaches of the schoolyard to sit beneath a tree three times a day *every single day*? And really, what sixth-grader with any sense of self-coolness brings a backpack to recess? Shouldn't that have tripped some mental alarms?

In a matter of weeks we must have covered Mr. Jorgen's entire stash, because Donny one day stopped bringing the magazines. Probably a blessing in disguise. Spending recess a hundred yards from the rest of the fifth and sixth grades certainly wasn't contributing to our social development. By the same token, I imagine how we might have turned out if a rumor had spread throughout the school that we were learning sex education not from the black-and-white filmstrip shown since 1953 (which would come the following year), and not from the soccer coach's painful explanation of the birds and the bees, but rather from the colorful teachings of Mr. Hugh Hefner. Having shared an experience that probably should have bonded us but really didn't, Donny and I returned to the playground and were welcomed back into the folds of society, two chubby targets for dodgeball.

After that year, Donny was transferred to another school and I never saw him again—possibly the victim of a father whose porn collection had been disrupted. But the Universe was not yet satisfied with my exposure to photos of naked women.

We moved twice within Camarillo, this time to Acala

Street and into a neighborhood where there lived a certain child criminal named Brandon. In Cameron's and my eyes he wasn't all that bad. But then arson of Matchbox cars wasn't necessarily "bad" either. Naturally, our parents saw a side of Brandon from a perspective invisible to us as boys.

"I don't think you guys should hang around that... *Brandon*," our mother told us, emphasizing his name as though it were synonymous with leper. "He's a bad influence."

"No, he's not," I argued.

"What do you mean, 'No he's not?' Every time he comes over here he's reeking of cigarette smoke."

"That's because his *mom* smokes," I said. Brandon did too, but I wasn't about to tell my mom that.

She huffed through her nose. "Well.... Just be careful."

"We will," we said in unison.

And we *were* careful. I carefully helped Cameron into a vacant house through a bedroom window that Brandon had found unlocked, and then I carefully pulled myself in.

The house was on Acala Street, only two doors down from ours, and had been on the market for quite some time. We had no intent of vandalism or other malice, we just wanted someplace new to explore.

The layout of this house was similar to ours: a few

bedrooms, couple of bathrooms, sliding glass door into the backyard. The difference was that this place lacked every piece of furniture, appliance, and electronic gadget standard to modern-day living. We looked around and quickly realized how boring an empty house is, even to a couple of boys who once found hours of entertainment with sticks and gutter water. There was nothing to play with, not a single match in any of the cupboards, nor a mousetrap in the garage. Our only excitement was the thrill of knowing we weren't supposed to be there.

"Dude, go check out the closet in the master bedroom."

That statement came from Brandon, so there had to be something good in there, but what? A starved cat? A severed head? Oo, firecrackers?!

Cameron may have seen an issue of *Hustler* before, but I had never heard of it.

Long before the Internet, there was a *pornucopia* of nudie magazines on the market, each requiring its own lack of imagination. And at 11 years old I had the opportunity to compare them.

Playboy, I discovered, elicits the attention of a classier gentleman ("I subscribe for the articles") who, theoretically, is interested in politics, short fictional stories, and a model's supposed turn-ons, and who prefers to imagine what the models might look like if arranged in slightly raunchier poses. *Penthouse* removes a layer of intellect and imagination and simply puts its models into those slightly raunchier poses. It skips the political landscape and combines the model's turn-ons with the short fictional stories into a pleasant little segment called *Penthouse Letters*. And at the south end of the spectrum, *Hustler* says, *Fuck that shit*, and shoves page after page of bent-over, spread-legged women in your face. And once again there we were, Cameron and I, and now Brandon, in an enclosed area, flipping the pages of nudie mags. Turns out, like Donny's dad, Brandon's dad was a collector, too.

When the police learned we were sneaking into an empty house (we did it in broad daylight, after all), we were called to a meeting with an officer, our parents, and Brandon's mom. Brandon supposedly had suffered an asthma attack and couldn't attend. *Lucky son of a....* It was the first time I heard the phrase "breaking and entering" and the last time I needed to. It was very serious, the officer explained. But at that age the punishment seemed worse: grounded for a month.

I lost my appetite for sneaking into places, at least temporarily, and for pornography more or less permanently. We moved to Idaho soon after, and my new friends' dads apparently didn't collect such material. Or at least they were better at hiding it.

A Martyr for Coolness

Cameron and I were specifically warned not to cross Lewis Road, which was the primary reason to do exactly that.

Our house on Acala Street in Camarillo was situated near the busy intersection of Lewis and Adolfo Roads. We climbed, sometimes with friends, onto the cinderblock wall that shielded our backyard from Adolfo Road and watched the intersection for the inevitable car wreck. It was kind of like whale watching: be at the right place and stay attentive, and you might see something spectacular.

A train track paralleled Lewis Road, and beyond it stood an office building and rolling fields of sage brush and dust. For many months I heeded my parents' simple warning to stay on this side of Lewis Road, mainly because there didn't appear to be anything of interest on the other side. But also because I hadn't been egged on.

"Dude, there's like a BMX track over there," my classmate Nate said. He shifted atop the cinder block wall, legs dangling over the sidewalk below. He lived only two blocks away, yet we had never hung out until this point. My lack of popularity surely was the reason for our lack of friendship.

"Well, let's go!" said James, my best friend at the time, ready to jump off the wall. "This is boring anyway."

"I dunno," I said. I peered at the train tracks that paralleled Lewis Road. The tracks lay atop a ridge, over which I couldn't possibly have seen anything. "Doesn't look like there's anything over there."

To admit that I didn't want to go because my parents said not to would have been to admit that I was a mama's boy ready to accept a demotion to weenie.

Nate continued, an encouraging slant in his voice. "It's pretty cool. It's like dirt trails and huge jumps 'n' stuff."

"Rad! Let's go!" James said. "Just leave the pussy here."

"Whatever! I'm going."

Minutes later we stopped our bikes at the corner of Lewis and Adolfo, and I pressed the crosswalk button. Suddenly, like the moment of impending doom in a B-grade horror flick, the intersection zoomed into focus while the background blurred away.

"Let's go, Pussy!" Nate called back to me, and I started across the street.

As I sped to catch up, I felt pulled in two directions. On one hand, I had my parents' explicit instructions *not* to do exactly what I was already beginning to do. I had also seen car accidents that took place on the very spot where I was now pedaling. And after years of abusing my bicycle attempting "freestyle" tricks like standing on the frame, ankles wrapped around the seat post and hands in the air, the brakes cables had wasted away to nothing; stopping required shoving the toe of my shoe into the space between the front tire and the fork. On the other hand: "Hurry up, Pussy!" If I didn't go, who knew the social repercussions? At school I had already distanced myself from other kids (i.e., my friend Donny and I were off looking at porn), and Nate and James were the most popular kids in school.

In the battle between social status on one side and safety, caution, and obedience on the other, if I was about to become a martyr for one of the two, there really was no choice. I pedaled hard and caught up to my friends, only to realize years later the true reason why the chicken crossed the road: ego.

The Callegas Creek area was a combination of what I had seen from my backyard—sage brush and dust—and what Nate had described—a dirt trail that wound over rolling hills and numerous jumps perfect for flinging boys and their bicycles into the air. We launched from several of these mounds with ease, "catching air" as much as possible, before arriving at the top of a hill. I pressed my shoe against the front tire and slowed to a stop.

The slope was fifty feet long, give or take a few, and leveled out at the bottom before taking a sharp turn to the right. Nate and James rolled to the bottom and came to a really cool skidding stop that looked almost rehearsed. I wiped the sweat from my forehead onto my shorts, got off my bike, and began walking down.

"What are you doing?"

"He's being a pussy again."

"I have no brakes, guys."

"Pussy."

"Bock, bock, b'gock!"

I reached the bottom of the slope and got back on my brakeless bike. "Let's just go."

I lagged behind Nate and James for a few more mounds and a few mild hills, thankful for the uphill climbs. Then we came to the next slope.

"Gonna get off again?!" Nate called from the bottom.

"Shut up!" I called back, and got off my bike.

"You don't really need brakes on these hills! They're not that steep!"

"Yeah, dude," James agreed. "They look worse from the top!"

I didn't reply, just started walking toward the bottom

of the slope. Nate and James turned and continued on the trail, holding my every chance at popularity like a carrot on a stick barely visible through thick plumes of dust.

A few more mounds and a few more hills, and I began wondering, *How far have we gone?* and, *If this is Callegas Creek, where's the water?* when we came to the top of the third steep decline. It was carved with the ruts of heavy winter rainfall and was littered with fist-sized rocks embedded in the dirt. Nate and James sped over the top edge without stopping. And this time so did I.

Martyrdom, here I come! My bike rumbled beneath me, tires slipping left and right over loose rocks. To press my foot against the front tire now would have been suicide. I tore down the slope, knuckles white, teeth chattering, and in a moment that forever will remain a perfect blur I was airborne. Without my bike.

When Nate and James reached the bottom they turned to wait for me, but instead dropped their bikes and ran back.

I lay on the hard dirt, squinting in the sun. My face was peppered with gravel and stung with the burn of road rash.

"Holy shit! Dude, are you okay?"

No, I'm not okay! I'm sweaty, I'm hot, I'm dehydrated, I've been called Pussy all morning, and now I'm lying in a bloody, dirty heap in the middle of some brush field I wasn't supposed to go to in the first place!

"Yeah, I'm fine." *Don't cry, Mikey, just don't cry.*

"Sit up," James said. "Gimme your shirt."

"No! Don't take off my shirt." James later ridiculed me for that comment. Here I was, my face a scab in the making, and my vanity, he thought, was preventing me from revealing my flab. Actually, my gut was the last thing on my mind. I didn't want the collar of a T-shirt scraping at my raw face like sandpaper. So James dabbed at the blood and grit with his own sweaty T-shirt, which of course scraped at my raw face like sandpaper. That's when I lost consciousness.

The living room where I woke was small and decorated with typical and atypical living room items: couch, matching chair, coffee table, TV, and some odd contraption made of two black, waist-high, tubes formed into triangles and connected at their top points with a stretcher-like platform.

"Dude, how ya feelin'?"

I shrugged on the couch. "Where are we?"

"You're at my house," a female voice said, and appeared from another room. She was young, slender, and soft-spoken. She placed a glass of fruit punch on the coffee table and replaced the warm, wet washcloth on my forehead with a cool one.

I tried to sit up, and immediately my face throbbed with the sudden rush of blood.

"Just lie back. I'll get you a straw. Your dad'll be here soon."

You called my dad? I thought. *Where'd you get his work number?*

The woman brought a straw and moistened the washcloth, then strapped herself against the platform of the contraption. As she leaned back, the platform tipped backward, standing the woman on her head. In my disoriented state and horizontal position on the couch, this looked mildly uncomfortable, and I wondered why anyone would intentionally turn themselves upside down...and stay there.

"Relieves stress," she said, as though she'd read my aching mind, and slowly returned to her normal, upright position.

She repeated the motion several times, and I turned my head toward the television, unable to watch her without empathizing and thus feeling nauseous. When the doorbell rang, James opened the door while the woman released herself from the odd device and ran her hands over her hair.

Dad stepped inside, shook her hand, and introduced himself as the father of the consistently failing suicidal on her couch.

"Nothing's broken?" he asked, and when I shook my head, he lifted me with a grunt. "Thank you for taking care of him," he told the woman.

"No problem at all," she said, smiling. "Get better, Mike."

Nate and James quickly offered to ride their bikes home, knowing full well that they had lured me into Callegas Creek.

"Good idea," Dad replied, assuming the same knowledge.

He loaded me into the back seat of the wood-paneled station wagon and my bike into the back end. I dozed on the way to wherever we were going.

"So you know you weren't supposed to cross Lewis Road, right?"

Dad had returned from phoning Mom and sat beside me in the waiting room of the ER at Pleasant Valley Hospital. Cases more urgent than mine were filing in and out.

"Yes," I muttered.

"And now you know why?"

"Yes."

"Why?" Dad asked, and removed his sport jacket.

"Because the brakes on my bike don't work?" I grinned, and then winced at the pain.

He pursed his lips and rolled his eyes, allowing me this one time to make light of an otherwise painful situation.

A woman in hospital scrubs appeared through wide double-doors.

"Michael Muuuh...." We looked up. "C'mon back."

When my brother Cameron removed the tip of my thumb with a breadknife and the doctor enlisted Betadine to teach me a lesson, agonizing was an accurate description of the experience. Now, however, it wasn't a two-centimeter section of a finger that needed cleansing, rather the entirety of my face, which was pitted with scrapes and gravel of various sizes.

"This will probably hurt," the doctor said upon examining me, and closed the door.

He laid me back on the padded table and promptly took to scrubbing the dried blood, sand, and insects from every nook of my face with steel wool dipped in battery acid. I'd like to say I took it like a man, but the squeal that ricocheted off the walls of the small room surprised even me. My face pulsing like the light at a railroad crossing, the doctor dipped a towel into what I imagined was alcohol or lemon juice, then blotted warm water on my abused skin and sponged it away with a dry towel.

"I'll be right back," he said, and closed the door behind him.

Dad looked over charts of internal organs on the wall while I lay on my back, staring at the ceiling through watery eyes. The doctor returned and placed a container of white goo on the counter as Mom opened the door. Her face soured as she entered the room and saw not her son but a hamburger-faced cherub lying on the bed.

"Now you know why we tell you kids not to cross Lewis Road," she said, skipping any empathy or standard greeting. She sat in a chair beside Dad.

"'Cau—'"

Dad's eyes caught mine: *If you're thinking about your little "'cause my brakes don't work" comment, just stop right there.*

The doctor greeted my mother, returned to the counter, and spread some of the goo onto a section of gauze.

"Is this gonna hurt, too?" I asked.

"Probably." He dropped the gauze onto the counter and took two tongue depressors from a jar. "Squeeze one in each hand."

"Well, he crossed Lewis Road," Dad began, looking at me but speaking to Mom, and continued to fill her in.

Meanwhile, the doctor smeared molten lava all over my face. *Don't they test this stuff on animals?*

But within a minute the doctor leaned back and looked at my mask. "We're done."

Immediately I noticed that he had forgotten to wash the goo from my face. Instead, he handed me the container.

"You'll want to apply this three times a day. Rinse your face with warm water, dry it, then dab it onto your skin. A few hours later do it again."

It had the consistency of Elmer's paste and the smell of moth balls.

"'Do it again?' I have to wear this stuff all day?"

He nodded, and his raised eyebrows said it all: *You shouldn't have crossed Lewis Road.*

"We're all done here," he said, and shook my parents' hands before leaving the room.

A day of disobedience and feigned courage: wasted. No one in the history of humankind ever gained or maintained coolness while wearing Elmer's paste on his face, or on any other part of their body, for that matter. And smelling like my grandmother's coat closet would help nothing.

"You know you're grounded, right?" Dad said.

A blessing in disguise, but I nodded as though I felt punished.

My mother looked up. "So how did you get from Callegas Creek to the woman's house, anyway?"

I tossed the tongue depressors onto the counter and pulled myself to my feet while trying to recall. "I don't know."

"You don't know?"

I thought again. "No. I'm not sure."

My father and I walked through the waiting room one slow step at a time while my mother called James. Stiffness was setting in throughout my body, and the goo was forming a solid mask. I was holding the hems of my shorts, which rubbed against the scrapes on my knees, as Mom caught up.

"Apparently you walked," she said.

"I *did*?"

"He *did*?"

"That's what James said. You got up and walked your bike for a couple miles while he and...what's his face?"

"Nate."

"Yeah, Nate rode alongside you. The woman was watering her front yard and saw you guys. She offered to help. *You* turned it down."

Dad rolled his eyes.

I didn't know how to respond. The goo was preventing much of an expression.

Mom continued as we walked at hobble speed toward the car. "She took you in, put you on the couch, gave you a wet washcloth. Do you remem—"

"I remember the washcloth. I just don't remember getting there."

Dad opened the passenger door and stood by me to be sure I didn't collapse before getting in.

"Hm," Mom continued. "You must've hit your head pretty hard."

"Good thing it's so thick," Dad added, and closed the door.

What Would MacGuyver Do?

When Chandra learned we were moving to Idaho, she proclaimed that she refused to live in any state whose name begins with "I" because not one of them has a beach and they're all populated with dorks. She was seventeen and allowed to remain in California to live with friends. Cameron and I, however, were nine and eleven and weren't given that option.

"But what if—"

"No."

"But how come—"

"No."

"It's not fair," I pouted to Mom.

"Life's not fair. Get used to it." She slid medallions of hot dog from a cutting board into a pot of mac & cheese. "Besides, you've never had any trouble making new friends."

"Mom, I don't *want* new friends. It's not fair that Chandra gets to stay here but I have to move to *Idaho*. There aren't even any beaches!" We rarely went to the beach, and I never would have come up with that reasoning on my own, but now that Chandra had planted the seed I was determined to make it grow.

Mom turned around in the kitchen. I was sitting at the dining room table, my cheek leaning on a fist.

"You don't even know what Idaho will be like," she said.

"It'll be lame."

She rolled her eyes. "You're right. Of course it'll be lame. What was I thinking? Sure, Mike, why don't you stay here? Quit school, get a job, get an apartment, and live like an adult."

There was no way I was getting out of this move thing. Of my available defense tactics, fight and flight, it was time for the latter. I grunted and stormed to my bedroom.

While Mom and Cameron stayed in Camarillo to clean up and sell the house on Acala Street, Chandra moved in with a friend, and Dad and I drove north to Idaho with a carload of essentials. Dad rented two adjoining rooms at the Best Western in Idaho Falls, and I became the new kid in the sixth grade at Temple View Elementary.

When the house in Camarillo sold, Mom and Cameron joined Dad and me in Idaho Falls, and Cameron became the new kid in the fourth grade. We were just starting to make new friends when our parents found a suitable house nowhere near our new school, and Cameron and I were uprooted again and replanted at Linden Park, the third elementary school we'd attend that year.

Being the new kid, introducing yourself to a classroom of piercing stares, has lasting psychological effects, not unlike your mom announcing to a store full of shoppers that your tummy's too big for you to wriggle into a pair of cool Levi's. "Here ya go, honey," she shouts over the dressing room door. "Try this morbidly uncool pair, instead."

My escape from looming eyes, pointing fingers, and pre-adolescent paranoia was lunch hour. None of my previous elementary schools allowed off-campus lunch, and our new house was only a half-mile away. In addition, going home for lunch meant that I could avoid the battery of questions crucial to starting new elementary school friendships: *What's your name? Where are you from? Do you have any pot?*

The arrangement worked perfectly. I met a shaggy-haired kid named Trevor whose family lived just three doors down from us. We'd leave from our sixth-grade class the moment the lunch bell rang, walk together to our neighborhood, and part ways to go to our own houses. I don't know how things were at Trevor's, but at my house Mom had lunch ready and waiting. It was like being royalty, meals prepared and taken in the privacy of home, away from the social pressures and din of the public arena. Thus the routine was established.

So when I arrived at home one fine spring noon to discover Mom's station wagon replaced with an oil spot, confusion and despair commandeered my expression.

"You can come eat with me," Trevor offered.

But how could I do that? I hadn't met his parents. Certainly that would be imposing.

"That's okay," I replied, and returned to my angst. *I can make my own lunch. Give Mom a break this one time.* And that, I believe, is the moment when logic and reason also took a break.

The front door was locked. We had moved only recently, and spare keys had yet to be made. I jiggled the knob but no luck, and no answer to my ringing the bell or eventually to my pounding on the door. The sliding glass door to the backyard was also locked. The garage doors: locked. The basement windows: locked. *Who's responsible for this?!* thought the spoiled brat. *I demand an explanation!*

I tried each opening a second time with no luck. Then it struck me.

What would MacGuyver do? I looked around the backyard for a gum wrapper or a paperclip or a misplaced hunk of magnesium and a magnifying glass, but found only a fist-sized rock, so I threw it through a window in the side of the garage.

The crash of broken glass was louder than I expected,

and I looked around for neighbors. Not a soul in sight. A quick unlatching of the lock, and I was in. I picked up the rock and a few glass shards and tossed them into the trash before entering the house for a boloney sandwich.

•••

"You *what?!*" Dad said. He stood his briefcase on the hallway floor and hung his jacket, while my mother returned to the kitchen.

Thanks a lot, Mom. My head lowered like that of a dog embarrassed by its own fart.

"You broke a window to get *lunch?*"

"All the doors were locked," explained the spoiled brat. "And the windows, too."

"Why didn't you just go to Trevor's?"

"I asked him the same thing," Mom called from the kitchen.

Pride, embarrassment, timidity, thoughtlessness, frustration, selfishness, and most of all my deep appreciation for getting away from other kids and doing things my way. Besides, I'd had bad experiences with food at friends' houses. Tuna salad with finely diced pickles, spaghetti sauce with massive chunks of onion, and in a word: liver. So there was a psychological *need* to make my own lunch. And truly I didn't feel like risking the social pressure of having to tell Trevor and his mother that lunch was great but that I wasn't actually all that hungry—in essence, lying—and then starving all afternoon if lunch at his house had turned out foul.

Why didn't I go to Trevor's?

"I dunno," I answered Dad, but I was too old now to get away with that response.

He pursed his lips and slowly blinked, loosened his tie, and trod downstairs to his bedroom.

"I'm sorry," I called after him. "I won't do it again."

"Pff! I hope not," echoed from the stairwell.

The window cost twenty-something dollars to replace, and Dad told me I'd pay for it somehow. There wasn't yet an allowance to garnish, but there were three large yards: front, side, and back.

The year before, Dad had taught me to use the lawn mower, but at the time I didn't pick up on the hint that he would assign the chore to me permanently. Now he saw the opportunity to teach me about lists of To-Dos and to stick me with this one.

The mower was gas-powered, but still required a human—yours truly—grunting behind it. And the edge trimmer, a wooden pole with a spiked wheel like a big ninja star at the end, also required a human—yep, me again—grunting behind it. We lived on a corner lot: the front yard rounded to the side yard, which extended the depth of the back yard, all of which was grass framed in concrete. Blisters were inevitable.

Mowing and edging the yards took a good two hours each weekend, but I enjoyed the work, actually, and the results. After being prodded to get out of bed before eleven on Saturdays, I poured sweat into the yards, edging the sides of the driveway and along dozens of feet of sidewalk. I never did pay Dad in cash for the window, but I did tend his yard every spring, summer, and autumn weekend for the next three years. I'm sure he'd agree that he got at least twenty dollars' worth of child labor.

The Marlboro Men

In a young boy's mind there's no such thing as a bad influence. He may go along with a friend's idea to explore a new place (trespass) or to accomplish a new feat (risk life and limb), and many years later he'll classify his boyhood actions as dangerous or illegal, but as a child the boy is unable to label the friend a "bad influence." The term's meaning doesn't even begin to take root until the boy's first chest hair sprouts, and by then much of his body is already riddled with the scars of having been badly influenced. He'll finally understand the term and begin to reflect on his own bad influences at age...oh...thirty-five, as his children are following their own bad influences.

Usually, such an influential person is older, seemingly wiser, or at least confident that the stupid thing he's doing is not stupid. Confidence Cameron had, conviction, even passion. ("Cam, professional wrestling is not real." "Yes it is! Now shut up, I'm watching this!") Age and wisdom he lacked.

So when he took me behind Linden Park Elementary School in Idaho Falls one cool night to "show me something," I should have reflected on our porn experience and labeled him a bad influence. But I was nowhere near thirty-five, and my first chest hair had yet to surface, so really I hadn't developed the mental capacity even to think in those terms. Instead, I accepted a cigarette from his pack.

"No, dude, put the other end in your mouth," he said. "You *light* that end." The tobacco was now wet with slobber. He flung the useless thing onto the roof of the single-story school, getting rid of the evidence, and handed me a fresh cigarette. "And don't drool on this one. Now inhale as I light it."

I did as he instructed, lightly pinching the Marlboro between my thumb and index finger like the amateur I was. But *inhaling* is not how an experienced smoker lights a cigarette. The tiny flame from the lighter bent into the tip, and immediately I coughed.

"That's normal your first time," Cameron said. He smoothly dragged on his own cigarette, then blew smoke rings into the still night air. I gave myself a minute to recover while he grinned.

You can usually spot a novice smoker at a glance. He'll be coughing, yes, but both novice and expert smokers cough. The difference, of course, is that the novice's cough usually sounds healthier, for obvious reasons. A more accurate test, however, is viewing the way the novice holds his cigarette. Most beginners pinch them, but they quickly realize that they're the only person pinching their cigarette, and they immediately do what most people do when singled out: succumb to group mentality. Soon the newbie adapts the cooler, more sophisticated hold, between the index and middle fingers, and is adopted into the smoking circle, now qualified to impart what he's learned to a new set of healthy lungs.

After taking the first several drags, I began to do as you're supposed to do, which is not to inhale, but rather to create suction in the mouth, drag in smoke, *then* inhale. But the filter was so close to my tongue that every drag created a burning sensation in a single, localized spot. I repeated this several times, drawing smoke into my mouth, feeling the burn on my tongue, and then blowing the smoke into the air, not having taken any into my lungs. I was unimpressed with the experience so far.

"How is it?" Cameron asked.

"Good! I just don't understand why people do this. It tastes like shit and my tongue hurts."

"For the buzz. Don't you feel it?"

I thought about it for a moment, searching my body for any change in feeling. "No."

Cameron was too young to explain that smoking cigarettes limits the oxygen that flows to the brain and enables the lungs to absorb nicotine, that these are what cause the buzz, and that if you don't actually inhale the smoke, you're giving yourself the gifts of wretched breath and foul-smelling clothes without the ultimate and only intended benefit of smoking: the buzz. So instead, Cameron shrugged. "Hm. I do." He took a drag.

We walked home that night, only one of us truly satisfied. Sure, I learned what smoking tastes like: it tastes like smoke, duh. And I learned the techniques for lighting and holding a cigarette so as not to look like an imbecile. I even learned how to keep it dry. And there was a certain *cool* feeling to it, I guess, but children feel that way about most adult activities. I could have been sipping Scotch whisky and listening to an old Dizzy Gillespie album or sipping coffee and reading the *Wall Street Journal*. While I wouldn't have understood either activity, I'd have felt cool just for doing something intended for adults. At least until boredom set in, about thirty seconds into it.

When we got home, Cameron had one more lesson for me: concealing the evidence. We buried our jeans and T-shirts in the hamper beneath other soiled clothing and showered before going to bed.

Brotherly Love

During the summer after sixth grade, my friend James came from California to visit me in Idaho and, unofficially, to help torture Cameron. This torture lasted three weeks and began with rigging Cameron's bedroom door so that, when opened, a pink plastic bucket would fall on his head. Unlike cartoon depictions, the bucket did not capsize as expected and instead dropped upright from the top of the door, beaning Cameron square on the noggin. It made a pretty cool sound, like only a bucket beaning someone on the head can make, but if scored by a panel of Olympic judges, the prank would have received a 6.0 at best.

Our torture also included a variation on a game often played in the car or at the dinner table called *I'm Not Touching You.*

"Mom, Mike's poking me!"

"Mike, don't touch your brother."

"I'm not touching you. I'm not touching you. I'm not touching you, I'm not touching you, I'm not touching you I'm not touching you I'm not touching you."

"Mom!"

"Mike, leave your brother alone!"

"But I'm not touching him."

Throughout this summer there aired a commercial for some sort of easy-prep dinner that spared the innocent lives of potatoes—an ironic marketing campaign for a state where "Famous Potatoes" appeared on every license plate. "Save a Potato" was the slogan for the microwave entree and was the very slogan that James and I adopted and chose to repeat to Cameron incessantly for the three weeks of James's visit.

Passing Cameron in the bathroom brushing his teeth in the morning, we requested that he save a potato. Spotting Cameron in the living room watching *Doogie Howser, M.D.*, we suggested that he save a potato. Watching him ride his bike out of the garage to escape us, we bid him, "Save a potato!" And when he finally complained to our parents:

"What?" I said. "'Save a potato?' What a stupid thing to say."

"Yeah," James agreed. "I've never heard it."

I didn't often spy on my brother or watch him do boring things, which is why I don't know much about his sleeping patterns. What I do know, however, is that as a child Cameron was a heavy sleeper who could doze off on the couch and twitch like a dog dreaming of a chase: a ripe opportunity if ever there were one.

Somewhere in the annals of childhood James learned that asking a sleeping person, "Where's your spoon?" will prompt the person to talk in his sleep. So when Cameron fell asleep one night with his bedroom light on and the door open, James and I saw a chance to test the legend.

But not before piling Cameron's stuffed animals on his head. The heat slowly rose within this heap of synthetic fur and cotton stuffing until the mound exploded, puppies and teddy bears soaring across the room.

"GET OUT!!!"

We waited about an hour before returning and knelt by Cameron's bedside to question him about his spoon.

"Where's your spoon?" James said softly, slowly, like a hypnotist. "Cameron. Where's your spoon?"

Cameron sniffled, smacked his lips, and wiped at his scraggly hair. "Sh," he offered.

"Where's your spoon, Cameron?"

"Shh, be quiet."

"But I need to know where your spoon is."

"Be...be quiet. You're scaring 'em away."

James and I looked at each other as though we'd just cracked a vault.

"Scare who away, Cam?" I said in the same hypnotic voice.

"The fish! Can't you see I'm fishing? Be quiet."

Cautiously we eased open the vault door and crept inside.

"Where are you?"

"The Snake River. Now shut up!"

Without warning Cameron's red eyes shot open. "GET THE HELL OUT! GOD!"

We ran into my bedroom.

"Mike! Leave your brother alone!"

And I did for the time being. James returned to California, and messing with Cameron just wasn't the same without an audience. The fact was that much of the time Cameron and I got along fairly well. Our groups of neighborhood friends played *Kick the Can* together, we toilet-papered houses together, and we discovered a condemned public pool and ignored the HARD HAT REQUIRED sign together.

By the time we moved to Colorado, we were 12 and 14, and much of our brotherly torture phase had ended. Much, but not all....

Perhaps Cameron had forgotten about the stuffed animals piled on his head and the scared fish in the Snake River. Perhaps he was just tired. Nevertheless, Cameron fell asleep on the sofa one night while watching professional wrestling, leaving himself vulnerable to what may have been my *coup de grace*.

Had I not seen the black ballpoint pen on the coffee table, I simply may have changed the channel to *Cheers* and left Cameron alone. But there it was, calling to me...

"Miiichael. Miiiiiichael."

I started with his mustache, dabbing little dots against his upper lip, and soon I had completed the outline of the left handlebar. If he were going to wake up at any time, I wanted to have finished at least one part of the creation rather than outlining patches of hair all over his face and leaving the middle of each patch unfilled. With the mustache complete and thick, I drew a line from his earlobe down to the corner of his jaw, across half his cheek, then north to reconnect with his natural blond hairline. When finished, the massive sideburn was black as night against his pale, hairless skin. He twitched, and I withdrew, but he settled, and I continued. Several long lines of black soon streaked the left half of his chin.

Some people are able to sleep on their back, head centered on the pillow with their face aimed at the ceiling. If Cameron were this type, I could have drawn hair on *all* of his face rather than on just the left half. Instead, I took a seat in the nearby armchair and willed him to turn over.

He woke a minute later and realized he'd been sleeping in the living room. He peeled himself from the leather couch and lumbered toward the bathroom.

"Are you done watching wrestling?" I called, using every ounce of my strength to stifle my laughter.

"Yeah."

As I flipped the channel and sat back in the armchair, I wondered whether he would look in the mirror or just do his business and—

"MIIIIIKE!!"

Big Man on Campus

There's an unwritten tradition carried from year to year, that when a young man joins a fraternity he will be tortured, both physically and mentally, for the sole and ironic purpose of establishing brotherhood between the fraternity's long-standing members and its new recruits. This custom is repeated every year at colleges nationwide, and at the end of the hazing period, known as "hell week," the new brothers are accepted into the house, and very strong, even lifelong bonds are established.

In junior high school it's called "initiation," and it's meant to create no such bonds.

Just in time to allay my related fears, Chandra overcame her states-beginning-with-I mentality and rejoined the family in Idaho. She had graduated from high school by this time, and through her years had gained confidence in her ability to discern what was cool from what was most definitely not. I was twelve, and being (or at least appearing) cool was everything, so I often consulted Chandra about the ways of the world. I was certain her experience and wisdom would ease my mind.

The day before seventh grade began, I sat down in the living room, where Chandra was reading a magazine.

"What if I get shoved into a locker?"

She looked me over. "Dude, you probably wouldn't even fit in a locker," she replied, certainly not referring to my height. "I mean...there are people in the halls all the time. Someone would hear you."

I sighed. I knew I was carrying a few extra pounds which I would have to suck in when passing cute girls (who of course would fail to notice my porcine cheeks), but I hadn't yet connected my flab with an improved probability of being singled out for torture. So far, her experience and wisdom were not easing my mind.

"Don't worry about it. Nothing's gonna happen to you."

I nodded. She was right. Of course she was right. She was older and had been there. Or she was blowing me off to get back to her magazine.

The most challenging part of the first week of junior high school was remembering which class followed which and which books and notebooks I needed from my locker (looking both ways before opening it). Soon I knew teachers' names, classrooms, friends' locker locations, and the correct school bus pick-up point.

Two weeks went by and things were good. I was settling into the new routine and sucking in my gut every time I thought Danielle Messinger was looking my way when...

"Get *that* kid." (Or was it, "Get the *fat* kid"?)

I heard the whispering and snickering coming from the front of the bus line after school. I stood near the middle among dozens of other students, yet somehow I knew they were talking about me.

A small group of ninth-graders made their way through the line, and I looked around at the schoolyard, avoiding eye contact while of course remaining casual and cool.

"Hey, sevvie," said a lanky, blond ninth-grader, referring to my inferior grade. He ran his fingers over the top of his mullet and came forward from the small group of older, larger boys.

"Hey," I said.

"I want you to give me ten pushups."

I could have said anything. "Shove it" would have been apt. "Here?" I asked. *Bright answer, Einstein.* But what could I say—I like your hair?

"Yes, *here. Now.*"

"No."

Junior high schoolers don't need much to attract their attention to something they can gossip about later. Naturally, all eyes were on me.

The Mullet grabbed the back of my neck, squeezing into the pressure points on either side, and then kicked the backs of my knees with his shin.

I dropped, hesitated, and with his hand still clenching my neck, I started pushing.

"One," he counted. "Two. Three. Three. Four." I listened for laughter, but the crowd was silent. "Five. Six. Six." A small circle had cleared around me, mainly just to give me room. Most kids seemed not to care or just didn't want to lose their places in the bus line. And they certainly weren't swarming in to help.

"Seven. Eight. Nine. Nine. Ten."

I stood up, my face burning red, my arms quivering, and my eyes about to let loose. I wasn't accustomed to physical...well, anything.

"Thanks," he said, and walked away, his locks tossing in the autumn breeze.

Dick, I thought, but said nothing. And the sorrowful looks around me proved that everyone else agreed.

In the coming weeks, I watched for The Mullet at the bus stop and in the halls. I waited for him to be alone. I'd love to have bloodied his nose or doubled him over with a swift kick to the crotch, or even just shoved him into the girls' bathroom. Oo, that would've been sweet! Chances are good, though, that my plan would have backfired and I'd have ended up doing more pushups, or worse. But I never saw him again. Lucky for *him*.

∙∙∙

There's an aging debate over the proper use of a certain term. When one's pants, or more often one's shorts, are removed from behind in a single, swift motion without one's prior knowledge, a majority of those familiar with the embarrassment tactic know this as being "pantsed." To others this act of humiliation is to be "de-pantsed."

"'*De*-pantsed?'" Chandra asked, and instantly her experience, her wisdom, and her ability to separate cool from uncool appeared like a lighthouse in a fog. She turned away from the TV in the living room. "That's stupid. It's pantsed. Who says *de*-pantsed?"

"I guess people around here do," I replied, referring to Idaho Falls.

She eyed my can of grape Shasta. "Well, people around here say 'pop' instead of 'soda.' And 'crick' instead of 'creek'."

"Yeah. It makes sense, though. I mean, the 'de-' implies *removing* someone's pants."

She looked at me without expression. "It's 'pantsed.'"

The thoughtful thing about pantsing (or de-pantsing) is that there's no opportunity for the victim to become nervous prior to the event. It's quick, like a ninja attack. One move—*FWISH!*—and the pantsee is struggling to return the garment to an acceptable level while the assailant disappears.

Twice a day, in the morning before school and again at the end of the lunch period, students at Claire E. Gail Jr. High were forced to stand outside like lowing cattle, sun or snow, by the series of double doors that composed the front entrance. The herd congregated there, waiting for the bell that would signal them to stampede through the doors, fill the halls, and bang lockers.

For many, this corral was a social opportunity, ten minutes when friends could gossip about the kid who did pushups in the bus line, and when you could see and be seen by everyone in the school. If a fight erupted, everyone saw it and pointed. If you'd drooled ketchup and relish down your shirt at lunch, everyone saw it and pointed.

Of the two lunch periods offered that semester of seventh grade, I happened to pick the one that all of my friends did not. Eating alone wasn't so bad. Students were allowed off campus, which turned out to be a pleasant escape. But there's a feeling of loneliness, of weirdness that comes with standing alone in the corral like a single sheep among six hundred head of cattle. They moved their eyes over me, wondering why I was there alone day after day. *Who's that guy? Why's he by himself? Does he stink? Maybe he's weird. I'd better start a rumor.*

I admit, I was sometimes bothered by standing there alone, suffering my mild social anxiety, but not bothered enough to do anything about it, such as, Heaven forbid, introduce myself to someone. So I stood there, twice a day, five days a week, alone and vulnerable.

And then it happened. The corral was quiet, a little *too* quiet, and a mild breeze carried the stench of someone's first experiment with cologne. I looked up from the grass to see the usual cliques in their usual places. But wait, was that a glance at me? And that? What's going on?

FWISH!

What the...?

The assailant disappeared, and I never saw his face, only that his shorts were on and mine were not. A fight may have been brewing in the distance, and condiments may have decorated someone's shirt, but at the end of countless pointed fingers were my tightie whities, aglow for all to see.

I quickly hiked up my shorts and avoided all eyes until the bell rang. *Only two and a half more years,* I thought, *and I'll be done with junior high.*

But what about high school? Won't it be worse? There'll be more people, bigger *people.* I'd have to consult with Chandra, I decided. Surely her experience and wisdom would ease my mind.

TP

Sometimes I like to imagine the origin of stupid things. When a crappy commercial appears on television, I envision a large, expensive conference table surrounded by marketing execs in fancy suits.

"No, no, that commercial would actually describe the product we're trying to sell. What's next?"

Mumbling.

"Okay, okay, I got one. Okay, there's this sock puppet?"

"I'm listening..."

"Talking to a woman at a bus stop?"

As the exec continues, the other suits are smiling and nodding. "Yeah," they say. "That's a great idea, Gary!"

Another jewel of bewildering origin is toilet-papering houses. When did this start? And by whom?

There are some pretty creative souls out there, but I question the stability of the first person who headed out into the night seeking revenge, armed with a roll of toilet paper. "Yeah," his friends said. "That's a great idea!"

As boys, though, Cameron and I cared no more about the inventor of toilet-papering houses than we cared, upon entering a dark room, that Edison invented the light bulb. TP'ing was already firmly planted in our minds. Our family had been the victim of a hit when we lived on Blue Oak Street in Camarillo, and throughout the years neighbors' houses had been similarly wrapped. So by the time Cameron and I were teenagers, we knew a good hit when we saw one.

"Dude, there's like 20 rolls on that guy's house!"

"Oh, at *least!*"

We had the knowledge; we had the allowance money; we had the target.

Tray Heidelman was not a mean kid, nor a nerdy kid, nor a jock. In fact, other than his notable shortness and perfectly coiffed hair, he was pretty nondescript. His father happened to be a local TV weatherman, and their family lived only a couple of blocks from my friend Kyle.

Kyle, on the other hand, *was* a mean, somewhat nerdy kid. Cameron and I arranged to spend the night at Kyle's house, and the three of us had already agreed to TP someone. The proximity of Tray's house to Kyle's was really the only reason to consider it. That and it had big trees.

Arriving at the grocery store that afternoon, we decided that, in case anyone asks, we needed a reason why we were buying 36 rolls of toilet paper—and nothing else. And we came up with the perfect, most plausible explanation: our uncle was going on safari and there wouldn't be any grocery stores where he was going. Foolproof.

The check-out clerk at Smith's grocery store formed a Mona Lisa smile as each of three boys stood a 12-pack of toilet paper on his counter.

"Whatcha guys up to?" he asked, and pulled an empty spool from the receipt printer.

"Just shopping."

"Yeah," Cameron concurred.

Kyle adjusted his wire-rim glasses with a habitual crinkle of his nose.

The clerk replaced the receipt paper and closed the printer lid. "That's a lot of toilet paper."

"Our uncle's going on safari," I quickly began, "and he won't have access to any stores, so we're stocking up for him." *Oo*, I thought. *Access*. Surely that word lent credibility to our story. And *stocking up*. Brilliant!

"Mm-hm." He scanned the first 12-pack. *Boop.* "Where?"

"Where?" *Safari. Africa.* "Zimbabwe," I replied.

Kyle and Cameron remained quiet. It was obvious I could handle this situation.

"Zimbabwe, huh? What does he hunt in Zimbabwe?" *Boop.*

"Uh, he doesn't hunt. He just goes."

"He just goes to Zimbabwe, huh? Just like that, up and off to Zimbabwe." *Boop.*

I shrugged and nodded. Who was I to question the actions of my wild-hearted, free-spirited, non-existent uncle who apparently was prepared for anything except the call of nature?

The clerk slowly nodded. "I see. Six forty-two." While I dug in my pocket, he continued. "Well I'm sure your uncle will be able to crap comfortably, thanks to you guys."

Laughter exploded from Kyle, while Cameron and I bit our lips, struggling to remain serious. Adults weren't supposed to say words like *crap* to kids.

I handed the clerk two fives, collected my change, and let Kyle and Cameron carry our uncle's 36 rolls of toilet paper to our bikes.

We had packed black clothes into our backpacks, and at two a.m. we changed and skulked like cartoon criminals through Kyle's back door and into the night.

The hit was easy and took very little time. Three dozen rolls of toilet paper are spent pretty quickly between three boys, especially when they have a plan. While

Cameron furtively shrouded the cars, shrubs, and garden gnomes, Kyle and I stealthily positioned ourselves on either side of each tree, tossing rolls back and forth through the branches and over the top like high-lofted footballs. The same passing strategy worked to cover the lawn.

The job was nearly complete when: "You got a problem." Clad in boxer shorts and a tank top, the local weatherman burst like lightening from the front door. Three ninjas dressed in black dropped their rolls of toilet paper and ran like chickens through an unlit field and into a schoolyard toward Kyle's house. After a hundred yards I stopped to catch my breath and let Cameron catch up. But Kyle wasn't with us. He'd been on the opposite side of the yard when the weatherman bolted from his door.

"Should we go back for him?" Cameron asked.

I thought for a moment, imagining Kyle in his last living moment: *'You guys...go on...without...me.' Gasp.* "No," I said to Cameron. "I'm sure he got away."

With that we continued toward Kyle's house, where surely we'd meet him and laugh off the adrenaline. As we made our way down Kyle's street, two headlights and a roaring engine appeared behind us. We booked it.

The Dodge Charger squealed around the corner, and we ducked behind a short chain-link fence. Yep, the chase lasted just that long.

If we had been smarter or less intimidated, we would have run in the opposite direction—or at least laughed at the weatherman's polka-dot boxer shorts—instead of standing there, listening to his threats and instructions. When he finished, we found ourselves walking back to his house to clean up our own job. His car crept beside us, but soon we approached the unlit schoolyard and field.

"All right," I whispered to Cameron, moving my lips as little as possible. "When we get closer to the field, run into it. We'll lose him there."

"Sir?" Cameron called to the weatherman. "Do you mind if we go across the field to get back to your house?"

Okay, we weren't the smartest criminals. Just moments ago we had sought invisibility behind a chain-link fence. But did Cameron just ask the man whose house we had vandalized if he minds that we make our getaway?

"You boys will walk on the sidewalk where I can see you."

Cameron offered me a hopeful look: *I tried. Any other ideas?*

When we reached the house I saw that we had done a damn good job. Streamers of the toilet paper once earmarked for Zimbabwe now flowed like veils over everything above ground: house, trees, mailbox, cars. We had done a good job, and now we would *un*do it.

The clean-up effort took far longer than the hit itself,

and with none of the pleasure. The weatherman stood on his porch, supervising every move until the last two-ply sheet was picked up. It must have been five a.m. before we were turned loose.

As we walked back toward Kyle's house, Kyle himself jogged up behind us.

"Where have *you* been?" I asked.

"Watching you guys."

"What?! You were there the whole time?"

He nodded, grinned, and adjusted his glasses. "Behind a bush across the street."

"And you didn't come help us? You're an asshole." I socked him on the shoulder.

"Ow! Dude, you would've done the same thing!"

He was right. But I socked him again, anyway.

Another victim from our junior high school had to be Ronnie Smitts. It was simply inevitable. Like Tray Heidelman, Ronnie was not a mean kid, nor a nerdy kid, nor a jock. A little prim and possibly a mama's boy, yes. And thus the other neighborhood boys zeroed in on their target.

Three backyards from our own, Trevor Connelly's backyard served as headquarters where we set up Tent City, a collection of three cheap tents, population: five. Trevor had introduced us to ice hockey the previous winter, so he, Cameron, and I had enormous duffel bags, each of which held 30 rolls of toilet paper and two cans of shaving cream, with room to spare. It was a massive arsenal that could envelop a 10-room mansion. Five boys, six cans of shaving cream, and 90 rolls of toilet paper. This was gonna be good.

"Trevor!" called his father from inside the house. "C'mon in for a minute!"

"Just a sec!"

"No, now!"

"All right! I'm coming!"

He was back within two minutes. He ducked into Cameron's and my five-person tent where everyone was gathered, sat on his sleeping bag, and brushed aside a lock of brown, stringy hair.

"What's up?" I asked, and zipped the door behind him.

He spoke just above a whisper. "If he finds any houses in the neighborhood with toilet paper on them, I'm grounded."

"Shit," whispered Cameron's friend Steven.

"How'd he find out?"

"*Someone* left their duffel bag open."

I looked at my unzipped duffel bag. Toilet paper beamed white like underpants through unzipped jeans. "Damn it."

"My sister saw it and told on us," Trevor said.

"Good goin', Mike," Steven said. What the hell? I barely

knew this kid—this *younger* kid—and there he was, ripping on me. But before I could respond:

"We're still gonna do it, right?" Cameron asked.

Trevor simply exhaled.

Ronnie Smitts's house was exactly one block away. Trevor's parents would have to have been drugged, blindfolded, and flown to Mars not to see the one house in the neighborhood that would soon attract attention like a fart in church.

"Count me out," said Tommy. He was three years younger (and ten years wiser) than the rest of us.

Trevor finally answered, overlooking Tommy's comment. "I don't know."

"C'mon, man," I said. "What else are we gonna do with 90 rolls of toilet paper?"

"And six cans of shaving cream," Cameron added.

We looked around at each other's prepubescent faces.

"We should do it anyway," Trevor finally said.

I nodded. "Maybe they won't find out."

"Maybe."

"You're still out?" I asked Tommy, who was shuffling a deck of cards on his Flintstones sleeping bag.

"Yeah. I don't want to do it." He pulled an ace from the deck and examined it.

Trevor and I shrugged. Tommy was like our little brother. I already had a little brother, but Tommy was different. He was so small in stature, he was like everyone's little brother, and we felt a need to protect him. If he didn't want to go, that was fine. He dealt the cards, and we played Go Fish into the evening.

The alarm on Trevor's watch sounded, and at two a.m. we left Tommy behind and stole into the night—four boys, three duffel bags, and not an ounce of brains among us.

We worked quickly, cocooning every inch of the house, the yard, the VW Beatle, the sapling. Someone later bragged about filling the mailbox with shaving cream. About an hour after we'd begun, the last sheet of toilet paper left the last roll. We zipped the duffel bags, stood on the sidewalk, and admired a beautiful, moonlit disaster.

When Mr. Connelly's voice penetrated our tent walls, it sounded pleasant, like he was inviting us in for waffles. He had allowed us to sleep till nine, which is early on Saturday when you're 13. It's especially early if you've been out decorating the neighborhood the night before. His expression, however, did not say waffles.

He was escorting us into the house like new prison inmates when I stopped him.

"Wait. Tommy didn't do it. He didn't come with us."

The others agreed.

"Okay, Tommy, you can head home. The rest of you, c'mon."

Even from a block away the Smitts residence was a sight to behold. A very white sight.

A light breeze carried a chill on the air, and the ends of dozens of toilet paper streamers fluttered like tiny banners. We approached and stopped at the end of the driveway. Trevor, Steven, Cameron, and I stood still, mouths agape as though Alyssa Milano had suddenly appeared on the Smitts's porch.

We spent the morning cleaning the yard, the trees, and of course the mailbox, while Mr. Smitts and Mr. Connelly micromanaged, pointing out flecks of dew-soaked paper stuck to leaves and decorative rock.

As if spending Saturday morning cleaning toilet paper from a lawn weren't enough, Trevor would be punished further, we knew, but the rest of us cleaned obediently, subserviently, silently hoping our parents wouldn't be informed.

"It's not coming off," Cameron said. That's when we learned the chemical effect that shaving cream has on auto paint. He sprayed it with the garden hose, soaped it, scrubbed it with a rag, and there it was: a giant, light green smiley face on the hood of their forest green car. If this symbol of happiness were appropriate for the hood of any car, surely a VW Beetle was it. Mr. Smitts, however, didn't seem to agree.

To my dismay, I heard very little about the job after that, only that Dad had come to the monetary rescue again and had the Smitts's hood repainted. Cameron and I were sentenced to two weeks: school, homework, chores, nothing else. And tent cities were thereafter forbidden. Looking back, that might have been our final childish endeavor, a last attempt to get away with something typically associated with kids. We were growing up, and soon we would have more mature means for expressing our stupidity. Like drinking.

Sisterly Influence

When Chandra moved from California to Idaho, our parents relocated to the lower floor of the house and gave her the master bedroom.

"Why does *she* get her own bathroom?" I asked. I shared one in the hallway with Cameron.

My father smirked. "You want your own bathroom so you can do your hair and makeup without being interrupted?"

Damn! He got me. Wait. "Yes."

He rolled his eyes and walked away.

Chandra's return to the family had a couple of indirect effects. First, Cameron seemed to disappear. He and Chandra were eight years apart and had absolutely nothing in common. In fact, they were often at odds with each other. Since Cameron had an established friend base in the neighborhood, he usually left the house in the morning, came home after school just long enough to drop off his backpack, then disappeared until nightfall, only to hole up in his bedroom until morning and repeat the cycle.

The other effect was that, with Cameron so often away from the house and therefore unavailable for me to provoke, Chandra began to influence me. She subtly expressed her opinion of the Guns 'n' Roses and Skid Row posters that covered my walls: "Nice posters. Dork." I, in turn, defended them to her face, and then questioned them myself. I began to question other choices, too: the crater-size holes in my jeans, the rock 'n' roll T-shirts, the black raincoat I had taken over from Dad and wore to school on sunny days. "Nice raincoat. Loser."

And the influence went beyond bedroom decorations and fashion. One starry night, Chandra and I walked to Linden Park Elementary, where I had smoked my first cigarette with Cameron two years before. We rocked slowly on the swings.

"So how come you don't eat meat?" I asked her.

"Do you know how they kill cows to make beef?"

"No." They don't teach you in school that they *kill* cows to make beef, only that beef "comes from" cows.

"A lot of places bat them on the head," Chandra explained. "And sometimes it doesn't kill the cow on the first try, so they have to hit it again and again."

Whether that's true I never confirmed, but the image was enough to keep me from enjoying sleep that night.

"There's a lot of animal cruelty in the world," she continued. "That's why I don't eat meat."

"Or cheese, or eggs, or milk, or chocolate, or—"

"Or wear leather or suede or fur." She nodded. "It all comes from animals. You should try it—being a vegan."

I hadn't thought about animal cruelty before. On top of that, I *was* a little pudgy, and cutting back on cheddar cheese and mayonnaise on sourdough bread right before bed wasn't a bad idea.

"Eh, whatever," I said, and signed up.

The next day I was energized to try this new vegetarianism—actually *veganism*—thing. As I did every morning, I ate burnt toast with peanut butter for breakfast. And as we did every school day, my friend Jim and I met at his locker, then walked straight out to the Domino's catering truck at lunch time and ponied up two bucks each to split a small pepperoni pizza. We were sitting on the curb across the street from the school campus, wolfing down a sea of grease on a bed of processed dough, when it struck me.

"Ul, I'm shupposed to buh a vuh-gan to-duh," I said, mouth full of hot pepperoni and cheese.

"What?"

I finished chewing, then repeated myself and continued. "It's a vegetarian that doesn't eat dairy products."

"Why would you wanna do that?" he asked, orange grease drooling down his chin.

"My sister asked me to try it. Thought I'd give it a chance."

"Oh." He looked at the gutter and back up. "So no more pizza?"

A half slice remained in my hand. I hadn't thought about that when making the commitment. "I guess not."

"Hm," Jim said, appearing mildly disappointed, but probably just wondering what he'd do for lunch from then on. Little did I know at the time that *I'm supposed to be a vegan today* would turn out to mean *I think we should eat with other people*, as though our friendship hinged on Domino's. Come to think of it, I really didn't see Jim much after that.

"Eh, whatever. I'll start tomorrow," I said, and picked up another slice.

•••

Chandra and I continued eating pizza—or to be more accurate, cooked, flattened dough with embedded vegetables. Cheese seems to be an intrinsic ingredient on pizza, like dirt on a kid, and often we confused Pizza Hut phone clerks with our unusual order.

"Wait, did you say '*no* cheese'?"

"Yes, that's right."

A moment of silence. "Are you sure?"

Chandra and I ate everything without cheese. Milk, eggs, whey—they all fell into the same category, Dairy, and it was off-limits. But in spite of the fact that there were dairy products in almost every meal I'd eaten in 13 years of life, it was a relatively easy lifestyle change. Mom did most of the shopping, so she did most of the label reading, as well. She also did most of the cooking (and pizza ordering). On top of that, there were plenty of junk food choices from which the natural dairy elements had been stripped and replaced by unpronounceable chemical compounds, which may have been toxic to humans at astronomical doses, but no one was batting cows over the head to get them.

Within days of my intro to veganism I began longing for certain things: ice cream, chocolate, something—*anything* with flavor! Having been an omnivore till that point, I hadn't been aware that non-dairy replacements were available for almost everything. What a relief! Non-dairy ice cream! Non-dairy chocolate! Milk, cheese, everything had a substitute that looked the same, felt the same, and tasted *nothing* like what it replaced. What the hell had I committed to?

"Hey! Mike!"

I turned my head toward the kitchen to eye Chandra walking toward me with a plate.

"Here, try this."

I hadn't yet learned that when someone begins a sentence with "Here" and follows it with a command, it's not something you would otherwise do. For example, "Here, smell this."

"What is it?" I inquired. I took the plate, and my head cocked on its own like that of a stupefied dog.

"It's a lentil burrito."

"What? What's a lentil?" I cautiously sniffed the wrap. Chandra may as well have said, 'Here, smell this,' and I would have handed it right back to her.

"It's like a bean. Just try it."

In spite of my other senses, I bit into it and immediately let the bite drop back to the plate.

"Too hot?"

"No, it's disgusting!"

"Oh, it is not! Just eat it."

"No, it's gross!"

"It can't be that bad. Just eat it. C'mon."

"No."

"C'mon. Please? C'mon. C'mon. C'mon."

"*Chan*," I whined.

"C'mon. Please?"

"Ugh. Fine."

She stood there beside my chair in the living room and watched.

"Is it getting better?"

"Oh, it's...just...great. Do we have any salsa?"

"Yeah. I'll get you a bowl."

"Just bring the whole jug."

I didn't know how long I was going to last with this veganism thing. Carob chip cookies, veggie burgers, lettuce sandwiches. Mom may have been doing the cooking, but I was doing the eating. It wasn't her fault that things didn't taste quite right. The body has a way of telling you when it disapproves of your choices. So when something tastes off, it probably is.

But, I reminded myself, flavor was a small sacrifice, so my commitment to the well-being of cows' heads and other animal parts continued through adolescence—a time when more than ever my growing body needed the nutrients I was going without. Whether my sacrifice actually spared the lives of any animals I'll never know.

Eh, whatever.

Black...with Red Trim

My brother and I had a lot of liberty as children. We may have been grounded from time to time for the truly ridiculous things we did, but generally, the rules we followed seemed to be set by other boys' parents. Rather than having a curfew, for example, we'd go home at about the same time as our friends because they had curfews, and we were left with no one to play with.

Our situation wasn't entirely unique. Many parents want to give their children everything they themselves didn't have when they were growing up. Our parents just took the philosophy a step further. If we wanted something that was somewhere within the realm of reason, with enough begging we often got it. *Dad, I want to play hockey*, and after several hundred dollars in hockey equipment, I was wobbling along the ice on thin, steel blades, wielding a stick, and covered from head to toe in padded plastic. *Mom, I want to play guitar,* I expressed, and although a few birthdays passed before I got one, the want was eventually realized.

When Chandra was accepted to Idaho State University in Pocatello, an hour south of Idaho Falls, our parents invested in a second home near the school for her and her cats and some promised roommates to help pay the mortgage. The roommates never materialized, but Chandra's leaving our house in Idaho Falls resulted in a shuffling of bedrooms. Our parents already inhabited the basement, so the master bedroom became vacant. I happily snatched it up, and Cameron moved into my former bedroom.

But the light yellow walls of my parents' liking had to go. I was well into my rock star phase, and in spite of Chandra's ridicule, I hung on to some of my memorabilia. And Guns 'n' Roses posters conducive to black lights simply didn't belong on custard walls.

"Dad, can I paint my room?" I asked.

He muted the TV and smirked at me. "What color?"

"Black."

His dinner fork stopped midway to his mouth. "Black?"

"Yeah. With red trim."

"If he gets to paint his room, I get to paint mine," Cameron chimed in.

Our father smirked again as he looked at Cameron from the corner of his eye. "What color do you want *yours*?"

Cameron thought for a moment. "Midnight blue."

He didn't choose black because he didn't want to copy me, we knew, but his choice was as close as he could get. Our father rolled his eyes.

"Black with red trim, huh? Why? It's gonna look like a cave in there."

"No, it won't. It'll look cool." I couldn't have given him a cheesier grin.

He inhaled, lips still cinched, and returned the volume to the TV.

I don't know that either of my parents, or anyone of their generation for that matter, ever dreamed of having black walls in their childhood bedrooms. There was something depressing and psychologically unstable about the idea. When Trevor Connelly's parents down the street finished their basement, Trevor had no choice about the color of his bedroom walls; three became light blue and the fourth sported a wall-to-wall, floor-to-ceiling mural of a white-water river scene. It wasn't his fault, but we gave Trevor hell about that stupid mural. I saw an opportunity to avoid such hell: black walls...with red trim.

Although my brother, sister, and I received much of what we asked for, there were things we went without. When moving to Idaho, Cameron and I, envious of our sister for being allowed to stay in California, adopted a routine of complaining about the Gem State. We didn't have any experience with or exposure to Idaho whatsoever. Neither of us had so much as written a report on Idaho for school or even looked it up in an encyclopedia, so our views were just a forgery of Chandra's. But our parents told us that Idaho had acres and acres of open space, and motorbikes may be in our future. Suddenly, we could do without beaches, our friends, or world-famous sunshine, and in fact we could replace them with mountains, strangers, and snow. And motorbikes. It was a false promise. We never got the motorbikes. But it shut us up for a while.

Later, at a point when we had outgrown our bicycles (and abused them beyond repair), the idea of mountain bikes was tossed around. Then we were caught toilet-papering Tray Heidelman's house, and the idea was shot like a prize buck.

Of all the requests I'd made of my parents up to that point, allowing—and in fact *helping*—me to paint my walls black would definitely place them in the Odd Parents category. Yet it became reality.

The master bedroom was on the second floor, and drivers passing the side of the house on Homer Avenue could see into the window. The ceiling remained white, but the room was unmistakably black, even from the street, requiring a double-take and inspiring the question, *Who in the world paints their master bedroom black?* And though they weren't visible from the street, my Guns 'n' Roses posters did look pretty cool.

The trim was done in solid red, and we didn't stop there. Mom considered this a project, a way for her to express that parental longing to give her children everything she never had. In addition to black walls...with red trim, apparently she never had a red filing cabinet, a black-and-white striped bedspread, or a black-and-white still-life portrait of a flower for the bathroom. Nor did she have a black rug or black fuzzy covers all over the toilet. I hadn't expected all of this and would have been fine with just the black walls...with red trim. But it all happened so fast. It was a flurry of painting and decorating for a weekend, and by Sunday evening my yellow bedroom had been transformed into the cave Dad predicted.

"Well, I hope you like it," he said, and pursed his lips as he viewed the walls, thinking of the five coats of custard yellow it would take to cover the black.

I *did* like it. And I'd never do it again.

Show-Off

If there's a man alive who has gone his entire life without earning himself a scar while showing off, I'm not sure he can legally call himself a man. During childhood, all boys are required (by law, I think) to abuse three things: their siblings, their belongings, and most important their bodies. The experience is what toughens us up. It makes hard statues out of soft clay, athletes out of lumps of flesh, soldiers out of boys...yadda, yadda, yadda, you get the picture. So, similar to registering for the armed services at 18, I was only following my legal obligation as a boy when I slammed my head into a wall.

After two years on the Idaho Falls hockey team, I was about as effective a player as I was when I started. My handling the puck was more often luck than skill;

my wrist shots inspired goalies to yawn while the puck was in transit; and although my slap shots were powerful when successful, they were more often a test of my stick's integrity against the ice. But I could skate pretty well, and I had plans to use that to my advantage.

P.E. class: junior high school's equivalent to elementary's recess. Other than being graded for physical activity, the notable difference between P.E. and recess is that, starting at the age of 12 or so, the human body stinks after exercise. Showers—or at least spigots hanging from a wall like a row of flaccid wieners—were available, but at the age when we were just learning that bigger is supposedly better and we had no idea how we measured up, most of us boys weren't comfortable being together in the buff. Besides, a little sweat was nothing a quick swipe of deodorant couldn't hide.

Usually gym class included standard activities like basketball, floor hockey, and every junior-high schooler's favorite (apart from the rope): ladders. This one has kids running from the end of the basketball court to the free-throw line and back, then to the three-point line and back, then to half-court and back, and so on till they've covered the court and wished sudden illness on the gym teacher. But on one occasion, with the completion of permission slips, we were off to the hockey rink.

I hadn't planned to tell anyone that I'd been playing hockey for two seasons already. Instead, I'd just show up, hop onto the ice, and tell everyone how easy ice skating—and, frankly, all of life—is when you're a genius, a natural-born athlete, and simply a stud all rolled into one. But I couldn't keep my secret when I boarded the bus, the only kid with his own skates.

"How come you have your own skates?" asked Alexis Marconi, the class's cutest girl. Long, straight hair, big, blue eyes, and a laugh as adorable as a litter of puppies. She passed in the narrow aisle and sat with her cute friends several seats behind me. "Do you play hockey or something?"

I nodded bashfully and looked at the floor. So much for bravado. She had delivered one hell of an icebreaker, too. Had I even known the term *icebreaker*, I might not have been so quick to piece the ice back together. But too much time had passed to continue the conversation comfortably, and she had moved on to discuss something with her friends—probably how good-looking she found chunky, shy hockey players.

Suddenly Blaine Bennett appeared and sat beside me. His hair hung just below his ears, and he wore a dark raincoat similar to mine.

"Hey, Mike. Those hockey skates?"

"Mm-hm."

"You play hockey? I didn't know that."

"Yup. Couple years."

"Cool. You'll probably lap everyone when we get there."

I smiled. *That's the plan.* And now I really had no choice. Alexis and her cute friends now knew that I played hockey, so I had to perform. And Blaine now knew, too. By the time we arrived, everyone would know. And who was I to let down what I expected were the expectations of everyone on the bus?

The class unloaded, laced up their rental skates (all but one of us—wink, wink), and hit the ice—many students literally.

And he's off! Mecherikoff darts across the ice, nears the corner, crosses one foot over the other, and continues picking up speed as he rounds the boards. He does it again, only once losing balance and wobbling for a moment. Then backward! Look at him go! At that speed and with that lack of composure he's sure to land on his ass and take out some unsuspecting classmates!

Soon other students spread out over the ice, obstacles for me to skim as I whizzed by them. Some had caught the toe-pick of their rented figure skates and slid on their hands and knees to a stop. Others sat on the ice and removed their gloves to tighten their skates. Either way, I dodged them like road cones.

Blaine had found the penalty box directly opposite the rink. I spotted him and stopped like a wild cat, eye on my prey. He was sitting on the bench, bent over and tightening a skate, oblivious to the eyes trained on him from across the rink.

The moment is ripe, folks. The path is clear. Mecherikoff closes his eyes, and steam issues from his nostrils. He's visualizing his move: the dash across the ice and the hard, quick stop that will bury Blaine Bennett under a tsunami of snowy spray. He fires like a cheetah, pushing harder with each stride! He's now at mid-ice! Three, two, one...

Zero was when my ankle buckled, catapulting me face-first into the boards.

Ooo, I tell ya, folks, that had to hurt!

A hard, flat surface will usually win a battle with the face. A hard, sharp, and jagged surface will not only dominate the battle, it will take prisoners. The door of the penalty box was open, leaving exposed the corner, a knife's edge of hard plastic designed to take the impact of flying pucks and body-checked wingmen.

The rich red hue of blood seems all the richer against white surfaces, and I noticed the first drop as the second and third fell from my forehead and froze to the ice. I didn't have gloves or a hat or even a Kleenex to help absorb the blood. A helmet, you ask? C'mon now. This was junior high school. So I rose, steadied myself, and slowly skated off the ice, covering my forehead with the sleeve of my dark winter jacket. Blaine wobbled after me.

Mrs. Brannigan, the P.E. teacher, met us in the warming room.

"You okay?" she asked. She held out a folded paper towel and sat on a bench across from me before removing the woven winter hat from her curly head.

The sleeve of my jacket was black, and in the fluorescent light the underside had taken on a rusty red from the wrist to halfway up the forearm. I swapped it for the paper towel.

"I feel fine," I answered. And actually I did. If a real bandage had been available, I might have asked to return to the ice.

"Okay. Just let me know if you feel dizzy or faint or anything." Her voice and movements seemed to quiver, as though I might be thinking *lawsuit*.

I nodded.

"I'm going to call your folks to come pick you up. Do you have their number?"

Dad's gonna love this, I thought. He sometimes commented about how many times he had been called at the office to pick me up when I was sick or injured. I gave Mrs. Brannigan his work number from memory.

"Blaine, please keep an eye on him," she said.

A man chipped the bloody ice away with a hoe, and the Zamboni made its appearance. As classmates staggered into the warming room, each winced at the red-soaked paper towel.

In previous situations where other children's eyes were all over me, like being the new kid in a classroom of strangers, a bath towel couldn't have absorbed all the sweat from my palms. But now, more or less of my own free will, I had bounced my head off the boards and probably should have been embarrassed (or unconscious), and yet these glances really didn't bother me. Instead, I secretly enjoyed the empathy and attention.

As I sat there looking at my sleeve, Alexis smiled at Blaine and sat on a bench across from me to unlace her skates.

"You okay?"

"Yeah. It really doesn't hurt. Probably looks worse than it feels."

"Mm." She nodded. "Can I see it?"

What? Whoa, hold the phone! "You want to *see* it?" *But you're a girl*, I thought. *Girls don't want to see blood 'n' stuff.*

"Yeah."

"It may be gross," I warned. "*I* haven't even seen it."

"You haven't?"

This place had to have won the award for worst equipped hockey rink in the northwest. There were no towels other than paper, no bandages of any kind, and worst of all no mirrors for injured hockey players to view their shiners and remaining teeth.

I shook my head.

"Oh. Well, can *I* see it?"

"Uh. Okay." I peeled away the paper towel.

Alexis cringed, but not like Blaine, whose face and voice shriveled as though he'd just mistaken a lemon for an orange: "Lleeyoo-yeck!

"It's not that bad," Alexis said.

Mrs. Garrison returned, and Alexis picked up her skates. "Well, feel better," she smiled, and turned. Her pink socks left moist footprints on the black, rubber floor.

"Thanks."

Mrs. Garrison sat across from me.

"All right. Your dad's on his way. You feel okay?"

I nodded.

"Okay. Just hang tight," she said, and patted my knee. "You need water or anything?"

"No, I'm okay."

She half-smiled, then stood. "All right, everyone! Bus is waiting! Chop, chop!"

The class sat on the bus until Dad arrived 15 minutes later. Meanwhile, I stayed by myself in the warming room, occasionally exchanging one paper towel for another and all the while wishing there were a mirror somewhere at the hockey rink. A boy just can't resist the temptation to look at his own wounds while they're fresh. (And later pick at them when they're not).

If there were a punch card for the ER, I'd have been

due for a free visit. Upon my arrival the admin staff would greet me with smiles. "Hi, Mike," they'd say, and punch my card.

And by now I knew the routine. We signed in and sat down to wait for the next available room, where we'd sit again to wait for the next available doctor.

"I'm trying to think of all the times you've been to the hospital," Dad began. I had heard this one before.

I looked at him from the corner of my eye as he continued.

"There was the time you and your brother were sword fighting in the kitchen."

"Yeah."

"And there was that time you flipped over your handle bars and got amnesia." He shook his head. "That was so strange."

"Yeah, tell me about it."

"Ear infections."

"Yeah."

"And that one time when you had that weird stomach pain."

"Oh, yeah, and they made me drink that green…sludge."

"Yeah, I wonder what that was all about." Dad's eyes became thoughtful for a moment before he continued. "Then there was that *other* time you flipped over your handlebars and broke your little finger."

"It was sprained, but yeah."

"What else did you do? You jumped off of that tractor tire when you were two and sprained your ankle. We all thought it was broken, but bones at that age are still pretty flexible."

"Yeah. Sorry to be such a pain."

He laughed under his breath. "Well, I guess that's how you learn about life."

I nodded and smiled. A man in scrubs came through a set of double doors.

"Michael Muuuh..." We looked up. "C'mon back."

Rather than being led to an individual room, we entered a spacious area with several beds on wheels and thin curtains with miscellaneous pastel patterns.

"Hi, there," a doctor said almost immediately. He was young and fit and overall seemed content with life. He eyed the paper towel. "Looks like a nice little cut ya got there. Mind if I have a look?"

The paper towel would have stayed in place by itself at this point. I peeled it from my forehead and offered it to the doctor.

"You hang on to that for now," he responded. "Mm, yeah. That's a good one. How'd ya do this?" he asked, and began scrubbing his hands at a nearby sink.

"He was showing off for his friends," Dad said.

I'm not sure why some parents enjoy answering on behalf of their children in situations like this. Does saying, essentially, *This is the dumb thing my kid did*, establish rapport with the doctor? Does it ensure that the doctor is aware who's responsible for the injury? Or did just *my* parents do this?

The doctor nodded and looked at me for a more specific answer.

"I hit it against the boards at the hockey rink."

"Ah, I see. No helmet?"

I shook my head. "It was a field trip with my P.E. class."

He nodded, slipped gloves on, and tossed the bloody paper towel into a garbage can. "Welp, ya ever had stitches before?"

And they're off! Wild Imagination in the lead, followed closely by Stitches In The Forehead, and Thick Bolts Screwed Into Each Side of My Neck right on their tails!

"No."

"They're not that bad," he said.

What? Did he just say, 'They're not that bad'? Aren't doctors are supposed to say things like, 'Brace yourself' and 'Do you need something do bite down on?'

Then he pulled out the needle.

"Go ahead and jump up." He motioned with his head to the bed on wheels. "Good. And just lie back."

I followed his instructions. Then, "Wait! Do you have a mirror?"

I had completely forgotten to look at the hole in my

head while Dad and I were in the car. I could have used the restroom mirror in the waiting room, too, but I was distracted by memories of father-son trips to the ER.

"You don't really want to see it."

"Yeah, I do!"

"Nah, ya don't."

"Mike, just relax," Dad said. "You don't need to see it."

Damn! All that blood for nothin'.

"Okay," the doctor said, and brought the needle into view again. "We're just going to numb the area. This is a local anesthetic. In a few minutes you'll barely feel it."

"Where's the needle going?" Needles always go into the upper arm. Any boy who's been to the ER more than a few times knows that. But he wasn't aiming for my arm.

"I have to put it into the laceration."

"What's that?"

"Laceration? The cut."

"You're going to stick that needle *into* the cut?"

He shrugged and nodded, and his expression spoke on for him: Well, yeah. Where else would I put it?

All right, whoa, whoa, hold on a sec. First, that's gonna hurt. A lot. And you haven't even said anything to try to prep me for that level of excruciation, like, 'You may want to use the bathroom before I stick this needle into your forehead.' Second, right behind my forehead is my skull. Where exactly do you expect the needle to go? And third, like all doctors, aren't you supposed to scrub the open wound with one of those green kitchen scrubby things before anesthetizing it?

My quizzical expression prompted Dad to intervene. "Just relax, Mike. He's a doctor. He knows what he's doing."

I lay my head against the pillow and looked up as hard as I could beyond my own eyebrows. They wouldn't let me see the *laceration* itself, but I'd be damned if I was gonna miss a needle going into it.

It's a weird sensation when fluid is injected into a place where there really is no room for it. In preparation for filling a cavity, a dentist inserts a needle into the gum, and then injects Novocain. The whole thing is monumentally unpleasant, but within a few minutes, most sensation in the area is gone, and drool is trickling down your chin.

My eyebrows now prevented me from seeing more than the tube of the syringe, but I imagined a bubble growing on my forehead and questioned how the doctor would keep the anesthetic from squirting out when he removed the needle. Unfortunately, the answer was as boring as him holding his finger on the tiny hole.

Within a few minutes the doctor was prodding the area, and while I could feel his fingertip, the sensation was certainly dull. He dabbed the area with peroxide, then threaded a sewing needle and went to work. And I strained my eyes to watch every moment of it.

Eight stitches in all, and a billboard-size piece of gauze was taped to my head for me to present to my mother.

In the coming days I attracted a lot of attention in the hallways at Claire E. Gale Jr. High School. Other children could scarcely hide their thoughts behind their expressions.

Hey, there's that kid who got pantsed last week. What do you think happened to his head?

I dunno. We'd better start a rumor.

As though an alien were trying to hatch, the laceration throbbed often in the first few days, and physical activity only made the alien angry. The throbbing, and of course the potential for further injury, made for an easy out from P.E. class. And after I succumbed to dozens of *Aw, c'mons* and showed the class my stitches, there was no need to play *Show & Tell* anymore, and my classmates left me alone.

Now this is living! I soon realized. If I had known a mere blow to the head would get me excused from class, I would have injured myself months before. But it happened when it did, and I milked it as long as I could. I kicked back in the bleachers, sipped a Coke, and watched Alexis Marconi and her friends run Ladders across the basketball court.

Joyride

If it doesn't kill you, it makes you stronger. If.

Like most boys, Cameron and I had risked our health dozens of times by the ages of 12 and 14, but neither of us had stayed overnight in the hospital; i.e., the body could risk even greater danger and still get away with it. We needed more.

Our family moved away from Idaho during summer break, and the neighborhood where we rented a house in Colorado was in development and miles from the nearest... anything. Chandra was 20, and though we'll always be six years apart, we'd both be several years older before she took any interest in her younger brothers. Further, even if there were other people in the neighborhood, Cameron and I hadn't had a chance yet to make new friends, so we had only each other to impress.

It was July 4th, and what did interest Chandra was a fireworks show at a distant public park that night. Cameron and I had better things to do than listen to other parents talk gibberish to their toddlers. (*Oo, did you see that one, Billy?* I sometimes want to answer on the child's behalf. *You mean that massive explosion right in front of us? Yup, got it. Can you change me now?*) Cameron and I didn't know *what* better things we had to do, but we'd find something.

Commands like, *Behave yourselves* and *Don't destroy the place,* had lost their effectiveness years ago, and the phrases were buried with goldfish in former backyards.

"Just don't kill each other," Mom called from the front door.

"We won't," we replied, eyes trained on the television.

Like dogs excited at the sight of their leashes, we scrambled to the front door and looked through the window.

"What are we gonna do?" I asked Cameron. Our parents silver Sentra rolled away from the house.

"I dunno. What do *you* want to do?"

I was 14 and salivating over the idea that my driver's permit was only a couple of months away. My mother had taken me driving on back-country roads before, but this would be different. With a permit I'd be driving with traffic, and pretty soon I'd be honking the horn and flipping the bird. I couldn't wait.

"Wanna take a ride?"

We no longer had our childhood bicycles, so Cameron knew exactly what I meant.

A devilish expression masked his face. "Where?" he asked.

"I dunno. Who cares?"

"Yeah! But what if they took the key?"

"Let's look."

We searched the key rack, the dresser drawers, the kitchen counter, all with no luck. Then, "Got it!" Cameron jogged down the stairs holding the spare key to our sister's car.

"Where was it?"

"Drawer of Dad's bedside table."

It was dinner time and we didn't care. The TV was on and we didn't care. The house could have caught fire and we couldn't have cared less. We raced for the garage, and finding it empty, we opened the aluminum door. And there it was, our sister's 1987 Nissan Sentra—possibly the crappiest, weakest, and (except for its red color) blandest car in the history of the automobile.

"Let's go."

We jumped in, and suddenly I was Mr. Responsible, adjusting the seat, the mirrors, looking all around for other children.

"Put your seat belt on," I told Cameron.

"You forgot to say the magic word."

I smirked like my father. "Please."

"Are you sure you know how to do this?" Cameron asked, and double-checked his seat belt.

"Yeah. It's really not that hard."

I moved the seat another notch forward and started the engine.

The Sentra was an automatic with the daredevil speed of a bumper car, able to roar from zero to twenty-five in just under two minutes. I slowly eased it out of the driveway, moved the stick to "D," and tapped the gas.

It began uphill, the tires rolling one rotation every five seconds or so.

"You sure about this?" Cameron chimed in.

I smirked again and hit the gas. The Sentra lurched forward and we were off!

We drove about three blocks and stopped on a hill in a cul-de-sac of yet undeveloped plots. This was the highest point for miles around. The plains of the east spread nearly flat as far as the eye could see. South and west the foothills of the Rocky Mountains rose from the ground. As dusk gave way to twilight, fireworks shows started up, their light twinkling in the distance, but their sound too far away to hear. We stood for a moment, watching as one show became three, then five, six.

"Let's get outta here," I suggested.

"Yeah, let's move."

I cautiously rechecked all the mirrors, the gas gauge, the oil pressure. Cameron rolled his eyes.

As we reached the mouth of the cul-de-sac, an SUV approached on the connecting street. Almost any driver would have recognized the quarter mile between himself and the oncoming car and eased forward without reservation. Those drivers who wouldn't are either too old to drive—or too young.

"What are you waiting for?" my twelve-year-old brother asked.

"I'm waiting for that car."

It neared and passed...eventually.

"You coulda made it."

"Shut up," I replied. "It's different when you're the one driving."

He had no choice but to take my word for it. Ego fully recharged, I got the car going.

I pulled into the driveway a few minutes later and tried to position the tires just where they were before, then readjusted the mirror, the seat, everything to its previous state. And I must have come pretty close. Other than five or six new miles on the odometer, everything was exactly as it would have been had Cameron and I stayed home, except the house hadn't burned down and nothing had been broken. In fact, unless Cameron has said something, this is the first time the rest of our family is learning about this.

In with the Out Crowd

Many people express themselves with clothing. A man donning a three-piece suit, a gold watch, and shiny shoes, for example, is expressing his wealth. A 14-year-old, long-haired boy in holey jeans, a faded Led Zeppelin T-shirt, and a black raincoat may be attempting to express the image of a rock star, but he may unknowingly communicate a second message, as well: I'm an odd one, to be watched—from a distance.

When our family moved from Idaho to Colorado, I brought a different style with me, a style I had been cultivating for a year and a half, but which was completely foreign to students in the Denver area. There were other not-so-conservatives in the crowd; Alternative music was becoming popular, and bands like The Cure, Depeche Mode, and Nine Inch Nails were influencing many kids, as reflected in kids' dark clothing. I, on the other hand, was influenced by Led Zeppelin and Black Sabbath, bands that had descended from their peak 25 years before. Fashion had been overhauled between the 1970s and the 1990s, so I had the disadvantage of outdated trends and was required to come up with my own—a job not suited to a junior-high-school boy who had no actual fashion sense and who struggled with identity for years to come.

So for the first week I sat alone in the cafeteria of Huron Jr. High School, just me in my rock star clothes eating a sack lunch. Kids occasionally looked me over, checking out the new face whose unusual outfits reinforced their previous impressions of Idaho, "the Weird State." I was a little lonely at times, but I was near the door and otherwise quite comfortable. Besides, I didn't want to meet anyone. Conversation with strangers felt awkward. But I didn't have a choice.

They approached *en masse*, eight or ten of them, as I looked up from my sack lunch. *Oh, shit*, I thought, and held onto my PB&J for dear life. If starting junior high school here were anything like starting junior high in Idaho, I was in for some push-ups. Or worse, I had heard of a fun little one called *Beep, Beep, I'm a Jeep*, in which the initiate is forced to push a coin around the rim of a toilet with his nose while repeating the name of the game.

"You can come sit with us, if you want," one of the

girls said. She was at the front of the small gathering and exhibited the confidence of a leader.

For a moment I sat wide-eyed and unresponsive, looking over the group of mostly girls wearing purple-and-black-striped nylons and black pleated skirts or faded blue jeans and The Cure T-shirts. They were an odd lot compared to the pullovers and sweaters that seemed to fill the rest of the cafeteria, and certainly not the type of wannabe rock stars I called friends in Idaho. But cliques were an intrinsic part of junior high school society. And if weirdoes like these didn't exist, I wouldn't have fit in anywhere.

The lunch period was almost over, and I needed a response that wouldn't betray the cool image that obviously had attracted these people to me. I was about to say the first thing I would ever say to them and, depending on what might escape from my mouth, we may be friends for a long time after this. Or not. *Make it good, Mikey.*

"Yeah. Maybe tomorrow." *Brilliant!*

"Cool," the girl smiled. "We sit over there." She pointed to a dozen empty seats across the cafeteria.

I nodded (coolly, of course), and after standing, looking around, and saying an awkward good-bye, meandered toward the double door as the bell rang.

Undies on Stage

At 12 years old I begged my parents for a Nintendo, and I was so excited when I got one that I immediately plugged it in and played Super Mario Brothers for four hours. At 13 I begged them for a guitar, and I was so excited when I got one that I immediately plugged it in and played it till my fingers hurt, which happened in about four minutes. The guitar went into the closet, and I went back to the Nintendo.

Other than certain finger pain, the difference between a video game and the guitar was that the former did not (at least when the games were simple) take much practice before the desired results were achieved. If you pushed the right-facing arrow, Mario's stubby legs would carry him to the right. If you pushed a button, those same stubby legs would rocket Mario into a jump absurdly disproportionate to his squat frame. With only a couple flicks of the thumbs, the little Italian was kickin' butt and takin' names.

The guitar, I learned, takes a bit more effort to produce something that sounds like anything from our natural world. Visions of rock stardom and women's undergarments sailing onto a stage quickly dissipate when the first few garbled notes issue from a 15-watt amplifier. Couple that with sharp, painful creases sunk into the fingertips from pressing the strings hard enough—but nowhere near fast enough to make a coherent melody—and impatience will overcome most boys. Thankfully, there was Nintendo.

Even having taken guitar lessons, I didn't want to play.

"Mike," my parents begged. "We'll pay you 50 cents for every half hour you practice your guitar."

If I had practiced for just a couple hours a day I could have cleared over $700 in just a year and gone on to a multi-million-dollar career. Instead, the guitar stood in the bedroom closet, and I went on to become an unemployed writer.

When my friend Mark Hegelsen enrolled in guitar class at school, however, I reconsidered practicing my instrument. I could have signed up for Algebra or Spanish or really anything that might have practical application in life, but why would I do that when Intro to Guitar was available? I borrowed my sister's acoustic guitar, which had gathered as much dust as my electric, and bought a book by Mel Bay.

But the aspiring rock star whose hair was already past his ears can play songs like "Sparkling Stella" and "The Merry Men" only so many times before he needs to move on to Van Halen's "Hot For Teacher." The electric guitar was pulled from the closet and dusted off.

In the 1950s a miracle happened that changed the sound of rock music forever: the power chord. This three-note chord (technically it's two notes, but who's counting) is the hard, crunching sound you hear in every popular genre of music that involves a guitar, especially rock. It also happens to be one of the simplest and most versatile chords on the guitar, a beginning guitarist's best friend—so easy to play, in fact, that even the highest and drunkest of rock stars can make their songs sound…uh, not bad.

I wasn't into drugs or alcohol, but I was into Black Sabbath, a 1970s rock band whose biggest fans *were* (and may still be) into drugs and alcohol. I, however, was attracted to the band for their focus on power chords; think back to the song "Iron Man"—chock full of 'em. I sat with the guitar on my lap, pressing play—pause—play—pause on the tape player, until I had strummed power chord after power chord through an entire song. Other chords followed, then other bands, and soon I'd shoot to mimic solos. There was only one logical step to take next, and the road to stardom for many rockers starts in the garage.

Before learning to play guitar, Mark Hegelsen played drums. We rolled out an old shag rug on the cement floor of my family's garage and spent an hour piecing together his five-piece drum set on it.

"Dude, go get your brother's bow," Mark said.

"Oo, yeah!" I dashed inside.

As though immediately we were about to perform at concert level, I brought Cameron's viola to our first jam session in hopes of mimicking Led Zeppelin's guitarist Jimmy Page, who was known to destroy violin bows with the strings of his guitar. I hastily removed the bow from the case and left the instrument on the stairs.

I'd like to say Mark and I played, but instead we made a hell of a lot of noise for not very long before the police showed up to deliver neighbors' complaints. We were beginning to disassemble the drum set when Dad arrived home from work, walked through the front door, and headed straight downstairs to his bedroom.

"Mike!" I heard, and went inside. "Did you leave this on the stairs?"

I don't know much about violas, such as how much one costs or how much weight one might bear, but when a 230-pound man steps on one, apparently it breaks. Cameron's viola-playing days were short-lived.

"Sorry."

Soon Mark returned to playing drums in the basement of his own house, and I set up my guitar where it was before, next to the tape deck in my bedroom.

Progressing from pretty crappy to not too shabby took a few years, as evidenced by the length of my hair. By the time I entered high school, now in Colorado, my lovely blond locks hung below my shoulders. They fit right in with torn jeans, my black raincoat, Converse All Stars, and rock & roll T-shirts. In my mind, I was already a famous rock star, roaming school halls and shopping malls, wondering why no one was asking for an autograph.

There are drawbacks to the rocker look, however. First, either you really are a rock star so you can pull it off, or you come off looking like a wannabe who'll eventually have to grow up and change clothes. And second, the rocker look triggers some of the stereotypes we place on rock stars, like substance abuse and disrespect for authority. The problem is that you may not realize these drawbacks until later in life, when you look at an old photo. *What the hell was I thinking?*

So while I thought I had the look of the greatest guitarist never to have been on stage, in girls' eyes I was the weird, quiet kid with really pretty hair that they couldn't stop braiding. And in teachers' eyes I was just a boy who looked like he was probably experimenting with marijuana and loose women, throwing all-night parties, and likely conducting séances in his basement bedroom, which he and his cronies called "the pit."

To enhance the look, or possibly as a joke whose punch line was me, Chandra bought me a pair of earrings for Christmas. A lot of rebellious boys in high school had pierced ears and wore simple, insignificant studs or diamonds that communicated *bad boy*.

Chandra's gift, however, could be defined as anything but insignificant. They were hoops, gold-colored nonetheless, and not little, bad-boy hoops. These looked like swollen macaroni had been glued end-to-end around silver dollars, painted a shabby shade of gold, and hung like Christmas ornaments from my ears. Yep, they were honkers. *Bad boy* was not the message they sent. *Arrr, matey* was closer to the truth. And this at an age when image supersedes all else in the universe and popularity is the Sun. Nevertheless, she was older and supposedly cooler. ("Who do you think taught *you* to be cool?" she often asked me). So the faux gold swayed beneath the natural blond.

In the spring of my sophomore year at Northglenn High School, flyers were taped to hallway walls advertising the upcoming talent show. This was my big break, I could feel it. I quickly assembled a group of musicians to play bass guitar and keyboards, but our band lacked a drummer, and we were running out of time. Auditions were just around the corner. (Auditions for a talent show: a pass/

fail test to confirm either ya got it...or ya don't. An esteem builder for any high-schooler.)

We selected a slow, repetitive, drumless song that would showcase no one's talent and was certain to slip the audience into a boredom-induced trance, yet somehow we made the cut. The night of the performance, we dressed like rock stars—jeans, T-shirts, Converse All Stars, sunglasses—and performed for our parents and peers. Somehow Kalvin, the keyboard player, scored a black-and-white photo in the yearbook, his eyes below the brim of a Debbie Gibson-style bowler hat borrowed from Chandra.

By the end of that school year, long hair had overcome my appearance, and my gender was being called into question, aided by the earrings, I'm sure. Walking into a hall during lunch, I watched a teacher at the other end stop a group of letterman's jackets trying to enter the same hall without a pass. "How come *she* gets to be in the hall?" one of the athletes asked, and pointed at me. Four heads turned. "Oh. Sorry," he said, as I neared him and passed.

A boy's male friends calling him a girl happens all the time. It's a minor and temporary blow to the ego, easily repaired by calling the friend something masculine, like "dickweed," whatever that means. However, being genuinely mistaken for a girl by total strangers who don't know any better is a scarring experience.

When an unfamiliar neighbor collecting his newspaper called, "Morning, ladies!" to Chandra and me, Chandra took the opportunity to issue a soul-borne laugh in my face that rings in my ears to this day. Rock stardom or not, the hair had to go. Earrings, too.

By the next spring's talent show, I had cut my hair and assembled a new band, or rather a new group of musicians who would play one song together for the talent show and then go their separate ways. And a drummer fell into the mix, so our options for cover songs were wide open. We chose "Stray Cat Strut," by the Stray Cats, auditioned it, made the cut, and performed it with little fanfare. It was a better display of talent than our previous year's choice, but still we saw no volunteers for roadies, no women's underwear tossed onto the stage, not even a photo in the yearbook.

The following year would be my last, and I needed to steal the show. I'd been playing guitar for four years and was actually making it sound like it should. Chandra later told me that one day she and her boyfriend came into the house and heard me practicing in the basement.

"Who's that?" he asked.

"That's my brother."

"Hm. He's pretty good."

Her boyfriend played drums, and even though I'd never heard him, he was older and wore a leather jacket, so the compliment sank in.

When flyers for the talent show appeared on hallway walls, I collected some friends and laid out plans. We would get the crowd going by playing "Man in the Box," by Alice in Chains, a grungy song with a few power chords. Charlie, a fellow high-school rock star, would play guitar while I sang. A minute into the song I would stop the show, complain about how wretched Charlie was on guitar, and he about my vocals, and we'd switch. This wasn't what we had presented during the audition, and later the drama teacher and director of the talent show confessed her desire to wrap her hands around our throats. Thank God for the protection of our litigious society.

In front of the audience Charlie and I bickered about who made whose ears bleed, then he handed me the guitar and went to the microphone. Victor, our one-gig drummer, tapped on the cymbals, and we burst into Van Halen's "Panama." The sound was great, the feeling was great, the outfits were...uh...also great, sure. Anyway, we were real rock stars, sweating under the stage lights, taking in the wild howls of our fans, and playing the music that defined a generation—albeit not the current one. As the curtain was closing, I tossed my guitar pick into the audience and waved as if to gesture, "Thank you, Northglenn!" before my imaginary roadies assisted me offstage.

The band met afterward in a classroom behind the auditorium.

"Dude, what was that?" Charlie laughed and raised his hand for a high-five.

I slapped it. "What was what?"

"You had your," he started, then doubled over in laughter. "You had your," he began again.

"*What?*"

He breathed. "You had your back to the audience during your solo."

"What?! No, I didn't!" I looked to Victor for validation.

The drummer nodded and bit his lip.

"No, I didn't! I remember looking at them."

"Maybe over your shoulder!" Charlie said, and continued laughing. "Dude, your back was to the audience."

Victor, smiling, nodded again.

I didn't believe it. In fact, years later I still don't believe it. The one gig on stage where I could prove myself to the world—or at least to the fifty parents in the audience who just wanted to see their own kid's act—and they got a shot of my backside during the most important part. No wonder the girls didn't throw their undies on stage. The guitar pick that I tossed to the audience probably hit the floor without a single soul clawing for it and likely ended up in the janitor's dust pan.

Charlie and I went on to jam in his parents' basement, but when college started, I moved away, and we grew apart. If I had known that my years of practice, of blistered fingers and sacrificed afternoons would come to this, and that this would be the last time I'd play on stage, I might have paid closer attention. Damn.

Halloweenie

Chandra likes to credit herself for the moments we share that are funny enough to be memorable. In the heat of a summer afternoon, I asked her, "Can I offer you something to drink? Water? Iced tea? A nice, peppery root beer?" We were hysterical over the unexpected phrase, but as soon as she reads this paragraph I can expect a phone call. "*I* came up with 'a nice, peppery root beer!'" she'll say, a smile on her voice. "You always take credit for the stuff I come up with." Then she'll call me a butthole.

Chandra also takes credit for any and all good ideas that strike either of us. Recently I suggested that we skip the chaos of gathering for Thanksgiving dinner and just go to Chuck E. Cheese's, where Cameron's kids could run rampant. I was allowed to keep any minimal kudos accompanying that one, because, according to her, that wasn't really a good, creative idea. But when I proposed to dress myself as Wonder Woman for Halloween, and the costume she created was a glow-in-the-dark, star-spangled success, over time the idea, as well, became hers.

In concert with this, I tend to be influenced and easily persuaded by her, like some kind of weenie. With her persistence, I usually end up conceding the credit to her for lack of evidence supporting my case. I'm fairly certain, however, that in my sophomore year of high school I came up with the idea to dress as a Hari Krishna for Halloween.

(*"WHAT?!!* You...! Pff. Whatever. Butthole.")

I confess that I wouldn't have gone through with the idea—*my* idea—if she hadn't helped put the costume together. We bought peach fabric, a latex bald head kit, flip flops, a basket, and carnations. No doubt about it, the carnations were my idea, too.

("Fine, loser, you can take your stupid carnations and cram 'em, but the costume idea was *mine*.")

It was a simple get-up, just peach-colored cloth wrapped around me and held with safety pins. In fact, I became somewhat envious of the Krishnas. How cool it must be to roll out of bed in the morning and put your sheets back on. Running could pose a challenge, due in part to the flip flops, but pin your sheets just right and I'm sure a light jog could be accomplished.

By this time I was well into my rock star phase, and

my hair had grown beyond my shoulders. We cut a small hole at the crown of the rubber bald head, pulled my hair into a ponytail, and fed it through the hole. A little adhesive around the latex edges and *viola*! Sign me up, I'm a Krishna! A proud addition to any airport.

I was mobbed upon arrival at school. Never before had I been so popular with the ladies! The carnations disappeared within the first hour, and soon I was flip-flopping alone through the halls with an empty basket. By the time I reached my locker after first period the basket carried two gum wrappers and half a Twizzler.

The peach fabric, having been repinned a couple of times, lasted the length of the school day, but by seventh-period English class my neck wouldn't tolerate the fake skin glued to it. The rubber head began peeling away from my neck, leaving little flaps of skin-colored latex flagging in the air conditioning. I had planned to wear the costume to a party that night; the glowing red skin on my neck vetoed the idea. Fortunately, I had plenty of hair and very little ego to work with.

At first, Chandra was disappointed with the decision—*my* decision—but the costume change gave her the opportunity to play dress-up with her little brother twice in one day. Just after dinner, I sat on the lid of the toilet at her command.

She started with my hair, teasing it, bunching it, spraying it, drying it, till it enclosed my head like the explosion of blonde hair I had seen as a child on the cover of *Playboy*. Axl Rose would have been jealous. Next came the makeup: heavy, thick, colorful. Tammy Faye would have been jealous. Chandra chose one of our mother's bras, all of which were circus-tent huge, and a shirt whose neck was just wide enough to angle over my mass of hair but not so wide as to reveal my total lack of cleavage. One of Mom's black skirts safety-pinned just right; a pair of black fishnet stockings; my gold, pirate earrings; and mom's gold sequin purse; the ensemble was nearly complete.

"Go get your combat boots," Chandra said.

"Combat boots?"

"Just go get 'em." She looked me over and burst out laughing as I stood from the toilet lid. "Sway your hips as you walk." A new round of laughter exploded from the bathroom as I sashayed downstairs.

I laced up the bulky, black boots, filled my purse with Starbursts, and struck a pose.

My voice was throaty and deep: "How do I look?"

An odd look of smiling pity gave way to a third wave of laughter.

A car horn sounded from the street. I snapped my fingers on either side of my giant hair.

"Step aside, sistuh. I'm Audi five-thousand." I swayed my narrow hips out the front door.

Scott and Kalvin, who had not yet met my family, sat in Kalvin's Chevy Citation beside the curb, awaiting an almost bald Hari Krishna. Instead, there appeared a well-endowed woman in fishnet stockings and combat boots, her hair a tangled mass.

"Good Lord, Mike's sister is *ugly*!" Kalvin said.

Scott nodded. "Y'uh! Damn right."

In winter months—such as, say, October—anyone parking in our driveway had to hit the gas in order to climb the steep incline. Getting out of the car then involved gripping the open door to keep from sliding away on the ice. But I was 15 and this was a new house. I hadn't learned these things yet.

From the car Scott and Kalvin watched "Mike's ugly sister" strut onto the driveway. In an instant her legs were out from under her, her gold-sequin purse flying, spraying Starburst candy like a sprinkler onto the snow-covered lawn. The beastly hairball slid a dozen feet to the sidewalk then stood, brushed herself off, and marched into the snow to collect her purse.

Neither Scott nor Kalvin so much as opened a window to offer assistance. Instead, they laughed till tears gathered in their eyes. To a couple of 16-year-old boys, this is the pinnacle of humor and could only have been funnier if it had happened to one of their own friends.

Then I opened the passenger door of Kalvin's car. "Hey," I said, and straightened my skirt.

Accidents & Opportunities

When my parents traded in one of their cars for two Nissan Sentras, I immediately jumped into the driver's side of one of our "new" (used) cars and started playing with the radio knobs, experiencing the emotional appeal and unique smell of a new car. Now, more than twice as old and fifty times more analytical, I need more than radio knobs to excite me. But I was 14, and the 1987 Nissan Sentra had little else to offer.

It did have one feature that deserved credit: insurability. Whenever our family's cars suffered any damage, the insurance money intended to pay for repairs was simply considered income and spent elsewhere. Thus, in the few months after turning 16, I became a cash cow for my parents.

Like all freshman drivers, I was thrilled with any opportunity to drive, even a few blocks from school to Taco Bell for lunch. And driver's ed. had taught me how to respond in the case of an accident. What it hadn't taught me, however, was how to respond in case of an accident with a Trisha, whose dark hair and deep brown eyes often lured my attention away from our Business Law instructor.

Trisha and I shared one class and occasionally some hall space between periods, but never anything as meaningful as a conversation or even a smile, partly because I was the biggest chicken at Northglenn High School (I mean, if there'd been a vote), but mainly because she had a boyfriend with a letterman's jacket. She also had a good two to three inches on me. Let's face it, it just wasn't in the stars.

SMACK! I had been inching forward at the edge of the school parking lot, waiting for a clearing in traffic, when her SUV rear-ended me. The Sentra's bumper was not bumped at all, and instead was cleared completely, allowing a deep dent in the trunk beside the license plate. The entrance to the parking lot was only two lanes, and we were holding up one of them. We had to do something quick.

Driver's ed. taught that, *"moving vehicles after an accident, unless otherwise instructed by an officer or in order to prevent further injury, is unwise and may be illegal in your jurisdiction,"* and that, *"after attending to any injured parties, you must notify the police."* But all that training flew out the window when Trisha handed me her number.

"Just call me," she said, and got back into her car. This was a woman who knew how to get shit done!

I stood for another moment, realizing I had never gotten a girl's number before, and I began imagining the opportunities inherent to car accidents with attractive women. Honking at the back of the line snapped me out of my reverie, and I got into my car. I'd have to think more about that later.

Inadvertently, and without having thought about it, "later" came within a few months. I was 16 years, three months, and seventeen days old, and somehow I had already mastered driving—coincidentally, just like every other 16 year-old. I handled every aspect of the road as though I had not been born but rather had driven out of the womb: three-point turns, parallel parking, holding the wheel with my knee while eating a burrito.

It was Christmas Eve and our family hadn't planned anything special; we would gather as usual in the morning over coffee and cinnamon rolls and flying shreds of wrapping paper. So for now I took the silver Sentra and its dented trunk and headed to hang out with my friend Michelle.

The school year before, Michelle was among the mass of black-clothed kids who approached me, the lonesome freak in the junior high school cafeteria, and invited me to sit with them. With her assertive personality and keen eye for those who lack fashion sense, Michelle may have been the one to inspire the group invitation. *Hey, who's that weirdo? Let's get him over here.* She was outgoing, flirtatious, and had a list of guys who would have run through the hallways naked at noon to go out with her.

Around the corner and up a hill, then down the other side I drove toward Michelle's house. White flakes swirled in the air as though my neighborhood were a snow globe. I turned the corner.

The cars of Christmas partygoers lined the curbs like the lights that lined the eaves of the houses. Up another hill, around another corner and down again...*wait, where are my brakes?* For three months and seventeen days my driving record was flawless.

I was going grandma speed and so was the car I hit. But the impact was enough to take out the Sentra's driver-side blinker and sheer off a seven-inch section of the bumper.

The couple in the other car got out and inspected the damage. It was minimal, but it was sure to be talked about at the Christmas party they were dressed for.

I had never been in an accident, I admitted. And it was my dad's car. I explained that I lived within a few blocks, and with their approval I left them with the double-dented silver Sentra in the middle of the icy street and started the short walk home.

You think about places like Mexico and Tahiti, the

Cayman Islands and Fiji when you're walking in the snow, about to report to your father that his auto insurance premium is about to rise. You then think about how much you have in your savings account and how easy it would have been to just catch a plane to a sunnier destination if only you hadn't earmarked those dollars for your next keg party. *Probably not something to bring up any time soon*, I thought.

I didn't know how Dad would react to this. Years before, I threw a rock through our basement window in order to get a baloney sandwich from inside our locked house. He was certainly peeved then, and that was just a window.

Head hung low, I told him the news.

He didn't produce much of a reaction.

"Is anyone hurt?"

"No."

"Does the car still run?"

"I think so."

He nodded. "Okay." And with that he had already accepted the fact and started to put on his shoes.

I called Michelle to let her know I wouldn't make it to her house. She'd meet me instead, she offered—at the scene of the accident.

It was a quiet, cold walk with Dad that night. He seemed to be giving me the time to think about it, to dwell in the mood for a while as if to say, *I can tell you feel bad enough about this. No need for me to come down on you.*

He shook hands with the couple whose car I had damaged, then with the officer, who arrived a moment later.

"Why don't you get the car out of the middle of the street?" he suggested, as Michelle pulled to the curb. "I'll take care of this."

I turned off the radio and turned on the heater. Michelle parked and took the passenger's seat of the silver Sentra.

"Hi."

"Hi."

"Are you okay?"

I nodded. "Yeah. I just feel bad."

She took my hand and kissed my cheek. "It'll be okay."

K-i-s-s-i-n-g

When I walked into my first grade class, I sat at an assigned desk near the door and looked at the blackboard and the rows of other desks. It was nothing like the classroom arrangements in preschool and kindergarten, which had cubbies and "stations," but no arrangement for structured learning. For the first time, at five years old, I felt mature, as though I'd taken a quantum leap and left behind those younger, unproductive years. *I'm finally in a grade*, I thought.

Eleven years later my attitude toward school was not the same. I didn't care so much about the structure or even my grades. At the forefront of my 16-year-old mind, really the motivators that got me out of bed in the morning, were girls.

Now there aren't too many boys in high school who

can be classified as womanizers. Okay, maybe there are, but I definitely was not among them. I learned pretty young about the physical sensation of attraction, the flushed feeling that races through your blood and causes your body to feel hot and your skin to sweat. Or is that just me?

This unnerving feeling seemed to be a natural chemical response to the sight of an attractive girl, like an allergy, or a biological warning system that would have served better if manifested earlier in childhood, right before approaching a stray dog or cracking my head open. It presents the same feeling as when you're caught shoplifting as a kid: your brain makes a run for it, and you're left standing there like the idiot you just realized you are, jaw wide open and not a thing to say.

The mere visualization of introducing myself to a girl and the resulting *weirdness* that raced through my veins were enough to prevent me from doing it. Even if I could've gotten my mouth to function, my brain would refuse to take part (though my sweat glands were always eager to compensate). In class my attention was often diverted by the flip of long hair or slender fingers playing with a necklace. But the instant a girl noticed that I was noticing her, my weenie senses returned and I looked away.

Then I met Kelly. Long, light brown hair, no need for makeup, just a very simple look that worked great for her. She was a friend of a friend, and maybe that's what kept that *weirdness* feeling at bay. For the first time my body was cooperating: my palms were relatively dry, *and* my mouth was forming intelligible sounds, even making jokes. This was amazing!

It was summer. I was 16, and Kelly was a year younger. We took advantage of my driver's license and her driver's permit and drove all around the rural areas far north of Denver, Kelly (illegally) behind the wheel of my dad's silver Sentra. In high school, this was effective dating: two kids getting to know each other, exploring new parts of their surroundings, and Dad picking up the gas bill.

You know you're in the middle of nowhere when you pass a shooting range. And several miles beyond it, the farmland rolled in waves and hills. In the distance appeared an object. A plane.

It was immobile, but it wasn't on the ground. This old, enormous thing, possibly a 727, sat atop a single-story wooden building like a pterodactyl on a robin's nest, its nose, tail, and wings stretching far beyond the walls of the little structure beneath. The windows were broken all around it, and the parking lot was webbed with cracks. This place was obviously abandoned and probably hazardous. We had to go inside.

It was a restaurant—or it was once, before an apparent series of natural disasters struck. The black-and-white-checkered floor had been reduced to shards of ceramic tile; diner-style tables and chairs lay on their sides; everything was covered in layer after layer of dirt and pigeon poo. I thought of asking Kelly if maybe she'd want to go steady with me, but something about the moment seemed, mm... not quite right.

That weekend I met Kelly at a dance club in Boulder. Her eyes lit up when she saw me, and immediately she grabbed my hand and led me around the place, introducing me to far too many people to remember their names, even if I had been able to hear her over the thudding beat. She then dragged me to an area upstairs with pool tables and a view of people dancing below. I was thinking water balloons, but Kelly seemed to have something else in mind.

Leaning against the railing, she turned toward me. Her eyes flickered in the dancing lights, and instantly I knew what she was after. The *weirdness* crept up, and my entire young life flashed before my eyes: porn, shoplifting, stray dogs, toilet paper, cross-dressing. Was I ready for this?

I had never kissed a girl in my life. I had never practiced on my hand or made out with a pillow or any of that stuff. In fact, I disappointed cousins and aunts when I turned my head so we'd kiss cheeks to avoid our lips touching. How in the world could I share a kiss with Kelly, this wonderful girl who'd drive illegally and explore abandoned buildings with me? I turned to her, closed my eyes, and...

"There," I said, and, *Shit!* I thought. It was one of those instances when the words that come out of your mouth can be easily misinterpreted, and you realize that only after the words are out. And this was only one word, so there wasn't a lot of wiggle room. *There*, I may have communicated, *I did what you wanted me to do in spite of my undeniable nervousness.* What I had intended to express was the feeling of maturity I'd felt when starting the first grade: *There, I've reached that milestone.*

I'm not sure what Kelly thought of my comment. She closed her eyes and smiled her little smile as though analyzing the kiss, then turned again to watch people dancing below, as though my wish that she hadn't heard me had come true.

A week later she broke up with me. Must have been a lousy kiss. Then again, maybe she had heard me after all.

Underage

The living room: a place in many homes where no one actually lives and few rarely even enter. It's often where the most expensive and least touched furniture is found, and where an imaginary red velvet rope reminds children that they are forbidden even to think about setting foot. The rope is removed, however, for guests, who are invited here for *aperitifs* or after-dinner coffee. This living room is usually situated near the front door of a house and thus gives the initial impression that the residents keep a pleasant home. Only later might someone discover the ring of dried slime around the bathtub or the faint aroma of some half-eaten thing that the cat left behind the couch as a gift.

The orange-, brown-, and avocado-striped armchairs that our parents purchased in the 1970s were faded and beyond repair, and the Naugahyde couch from the same era bore so many microscopic cracks that it no longer resembled leather at all but rather some kind of brown, soggy cheese. Through years of exposure to children and interstate moves, the finish on the corners of two wooden end tables had worn off, and the legs of the coffee table trembled under the weight of a mug. If furniture years are anything like dog years, this stuff moaned to be put to sleep. Instead, it was donated to Good Will Industries, who would unburden us of it for free. Thus, for about two years our living room was not a museum but an empty space, decorated only with off-white carpet.

    The dining and living rooms in this Colorado house were one big, connected area, defined only by a chandelier, which dangled from the vaulted ceiling like a giant glass spider on a gold chain. This lamp's placement next to the kitchen seemed to make this the logical space for the dining room table, leaving the remainder of the barren space to the imagination. I imagined keg parties.

...

    In recent years, Dad and I have talked about his enabling tendencies. "Enabling" sounds like a positive, like something all parents would want to do for their children. It involves giving or doing something that helps the child in the immediate situation; for example, enabling him to paint his bedroom black. The drawback, however, is that the child learns the wrong lesson. Rather than learning to do something for himself, or learning patience because he simply can't do it himself, he learns that the parent will do it for him.

When a non-enabling father is approached by his 17-year-old son with the question, "Can I have a keg party at the house?" the parent replies, "Of course not, stupid. You're not 21." When the same is asked of an enabling parent, however, "A what?" is the answer, and the son's underage foot is in the door.

"A party. Ya know, a few friends hanging out at the house. There's no furniture in the living room, so..."

Dad's paternal lips began to cinch. "Will there be drinking?"

At the time, neither of us knew that he'd actually be buying the keg.

I shrugged my shoulders. "Probably."

"And where do you expect Mom and me to be while this is going on?"

"Oh, you could be here," I said, subtle emphasis on *here, in his bedroom*, where he sat in a rocking chair, lacing his sneakers. "If you wanted to be."

Dad had a certain expression while in the act of enabling: a smirk. *I don't really approve of this*, the smirk communicated, *but I'm not going to tell you no*.

"When?"

"This weekend? Saturday?"

His smirk returned, his eyebrows raised, and his expression said it all: *You're responsible if anything goes wrong.*

"You're responsible if anything goes wrong," he then said.

"I know." A solemn, serious expression covered my face like a mask. Actually, I knew damn well that he'd cover my ass if anything went awry.

"All right," he said.

"Thanks, Dad," and I dialed the phone.

By mid-week, word had gotten around to the 1,400 kids at Northglenn High School that Mecherikoff would be having a party on Saturday.

"Who the hell's Muuush...whatever?" 1,375 asked.

Thus about 25 people showed up.

"Dad, I have a bit of a problem," our next conversation began. Its flow was similar to our previous conversation, and its result was Dad and me driving to the liquor store the afternoon of the party. I gave him cash, and he came out 10 minutes later with a thick man in a back-support belt hauling a keg on a dolly under several bags of ice and a sleeve of plastic cups.

"Did you remember the tap?" I asked Dad.

He smirked and tossed it onto the back seat.

The first time we went through this routine we discovered another drawback to the silver Sentra: the keg may have fit in the trunk, had the car not been rear-ended. The man with the back belt heaved the keg into the back seat, where I stood it upright and buckled it in as though it were my own grossly overweight child.

Dad rolled his eyes and got into the passenger's seat.

The extra 160 pounds sloshing around in the back seat made a difference in the handling of the featherweight car. I braked early at traffic lights and around corners, checking the rearview mirror like a parent ensuring his grossly overweight child was okay.

When we got home, we lugged the keg into the garage.

"What are you gonna do with it now?" Dad asked.

I dragged an empty garbage can across the garage, dumped a bag of ice into it, and turned it on its side. Seeing where this was going, Dad raised his eyebrows, appearing to be impressed with my creativity. Cooling a keg inside an ice-filled garbage can has been going on at house and frat parties for...oh...thousands of years, but I said nothing and let Dad believe what he did.

Cars started to arrive at around eight, and I took a last look over the house to ensure everything was in place. The keg was in the garage, the living room was void of furniture. All set.

At nine the garage was raucous with laughter and chatter, while the bare living room remained relatively empty.

At ten the garage was raucous with laughter at things that aren't funny and chatter about sex, while the living room remained relatively empty.

At eleven the garage reeked of smoke and was raucous with bellows, slurred speech, and philosophical chatter, while in the living room some guys had found a deck of cards and were cross-legged on the floor playing a drinking game called Asshole.

By twelve the keg was still half full, but the garage was relatively empty. Girls and boys who had arrived separately were rolling around on the living room floor together. Then Marty Blick appeared.

Marty was a different one, to say the least. A burst of blond hair, a pale hue to his skin, and a red jacket with snaps up the front and elastic around the waist. While most people wave and say hello or shake hands when initiating conversation, Marty's approach was closer to an ambush. He began from behind, pinching the fingertips of his right hand together. As his victim turned around, the fingers exploded open in his face: "POW!"

Marty stank so heavily of gin by this point that a greeting from him, not to mention his standing upright, was a miracle. *POW!* had come out *B'AH*, and his exploding finger gesture nearly took out my left eye. In his non-exploding hand he wrung the neck of a half-drunk bottle of Gilbey's-brand gin.

"Where'd you get that?" I asked him.

"BROUGHT IT."

"Did you drink all that tonight?"

He wavered and looked at the bottle. "I DUNNO," he blurted. "I THI—I THINK SO."

Had Marty been born 500 years ago, his natural dislike for mainstream...anything and his booming, nasal voice would have made him a good pirate. Especially his voice. His sinus cavity must have been huge and his throat lined with wax paper.

"Can I see it?"

"WHAT?!" he barked.

"The gin."

He looked at it again. "WHY?!"

I explained that he'd probably had enough. Like any good pirate, he argued. Then he handed it to me, eyes never leaving the bottle.

"HERE. DON'T LET IT...IT OUT OF...YOUR...SIGHT." With that, he caught the banister, ran his shoulder along the wall, and eventually made it to the bathroom. I took the bottle to the refrigerator in the garage.

Marty spent the next hour tripping around the house in search of his Gilbey's gin. I tried to convince him that he had finished it. He may have been drunk, but he wasn't stupid.

He wandered into the front yard and looked inside the pink bucket I had once rigged atop my brother's bedroom door to fall onto his head. The bucket was empty.

"Blick!" a voice called from the open garage door, and a look of slurred hope crossed Marty's face as he turned.

I looked away for only a moment, just long enough for a crowd of drunken high school kids to begin gathering on the driveway. Marty put the pink bucket on his head and wandered off into the neighborhood. I checked my watch. 1:30am.

"What's he doing?" I asked.

A random, laughing voice: "We told him we'd give him his gin back if he went down the street with the bucket on his head."

Instead, Marty staggered to a neighbor's house, gently set the bucket on the driveway, and climbed into their Chevy Suburban. For five solid minutes Marty Blick pretended he was driving this behemoth thing, merrily shifting gears and pretending to turn what we knew was a locked steering wheel. Finally he got out, returned the bucket to his head, and staggered back. And like any caring and responsible host whose friend had had far too much to drink, I grabbed a camera.

He panted up the steep lawn, the rim of the bucket just above his left eye, and I snapped a picture.

By Monday when we returned to school, the name Marty Blick would no longer be heard. Instead, Gilbey the Bucket Head would attend classes in his place. And soon the nickname would be shortened to simply Gilbey.

For now, though, Marty marched up to me, bucket in hand, wheezed, and took a deep breath.

"NOW WHERE'S MY GIN?!"

Some people show gradual signs of intoxication: increased chatter and boisterous laughter leading the way to an inability to walk, and finally sleeping with ugly people. Others go from one extreme to the other, to all appearances sober for hours, and then suddenly hammered like a bent nail.

I tend toward the bent-nail category. So while Gilbey the Bucket Head was earning his nickname, I was upright and speaking coherently. And then it hit me. Suddenly I needed to get away from the smoke in the garage and the kids making out in the living room.

Kalvin and Jessie, a couple during high school, had holed themselves up in my bedroom, sitting cross-legged on the floor. I stumbled between them to my waterbed (yep, waterbed) and then I, too, sat cross-legged. They stopped their chat to examine me.

"Are you okay?" Kalvin asked, beginning to crack a smile.

I had almost answered when the wave I'd created when sitting down came barreling back at me with just enough force to shove me and my total lack of motor skills off the end of the bed.

"You just sat there, didn't move a muscle," Kalvin said

later. "And then you just tipped over. It was the funniest thing I'd ever seen! I mean, since you slid down your driveway in drag."

I mashed my face against the carpet and knocked a leg against the dresser. As I slowly righted myself, my stomach decided that rising at all would result in revolt. So instead, I crawled to the door, fumbled with the knob, and continued to the landing at the top of the stairs. I reached for the bathroom door.

Locked. *Shit*. Some moron friend of mine had probably passed out with the light on. The same bathroom was connected to the master bedroom with a non-locking door. I was piss-drunk and crawling and deciding which would be worse: creeping into my parents' bedroom on all fours or surprising them with a mixture of veggie burgers, bile and a whole lotta beer right outside their bedroom door. If I opted for the latter, one of them would certainly discover the mess with a bare foot at around three a.m., right after finding my moron friend passed out in their bathroom.

Like a villain in a markedly bad horror flick, I slowly turned the knob and opened the door to the master bedroom. From my vantage point on the floor I saw where Dad's bent knees propped up the bedspread. I crawled into the room and ever so quietly turned the bathroom doorknob. The door opened without a sound.

And there sat my mother on the toilet, burning a look of morbid astonishment into my memory. Looking back, her expression reminds me of the incredulous scowl on the face of Ghostbusters' Stay-Puft Marshmallow Man right before he exploded: he was *pissed*.

As Dad snorted and snurfled in his sleep, I dashed out of the master bedroom, rolled down the stairs, and landed myself in the other bathroom just in time for my stomach to stage its *coup d'état*. A moment later I understood how someone can feel a thousand times better the instant after it all comes out.

The next morning I woke at somewhere after five a.m. in the pitch black and on the floor of the windowless bathroom. As I rose, the carpet tugged like Velcro at the cut on my leg. *The dresser*, I remembered, and turned on the light to see a small strip of blood that had crusted into the carpet. *It's not going anywhere. I'll clean it up later*, I reasoned, and dragged myself to my bedroom.

After that night, Mom and I reached a new level of communication: silent understanding. It wasn't the kind that some refer to as chemistry, or the kind that comes from two people looking at each other a certain way and knowing what each other is thinking. It was the kind that says, *As long as neither of us ever broaches that subject, we'll never have to come to terms with it*. And we respected that understanding for many, many years.

www.NowhereNearManhood.com

Acknowledgments

My utmost gratitude goes to…

…my dad, a.k.a. "Dave," for a childhood with few (respected) boundaries and for his support in my every legal and occasional illegal endeavor.

…My sister, Chandra, for her honest feedback ("Nice raincoat, loser"), empathic advice ("You should try it—being a vegan"), undying support ("Don't worry about it. Nothing's gonna happen to you"), and playful jabs ("Now put down your Barbies and come answer the phone!") that continue to this day and for reading my manuscript drafts front to back about a thousand times.

…Scott Dace for giving up his cafeteria seat in ninth grade and for so many more life-changing moments.

...Corrin Burke, my lifelong friend, supporter, and inspiration.

...Randy Cohen, whose generous nature and genuine laughter continue to feed a wonderful friendship.

...Jason & Kristin Suchomel, who foster both the boy and the man in me.

...Christine Bennett for being a wonderful friend, a talented book and website designer, and a prolific smartass.

...Amy Ferreira for coaxing Scott to rent that porn movie and for myriad other funny memories.

...Felipe Botero, whose encouragement means so much.

...Justin Armstrong, Josi and Nirvan Khokhani, and Cairn magazine (www.cairnmag.com) for the opportunity to contribute.

And to my mother, whose fits of perpetual laughter would have been the perfect reaction to the episodes in this book. May you sing with the angels.

I'd also like to thank Cheryl Smith, Cassie Ward,

Nicole Chiantello, Kylie Wilson, Mary Johnson, Joslynn Badders, David Gibbs, Yvonne Trask, and Rob Gibson for reading the manuscript and giving their honest feedback and encouragement. Without them, this book wouldn't be the same.

Finally, thank you, dear reader, for reading *Nowhere Near Manhood*, for recommending it to coworkers, friends, and relatives, and for stepping back in time with me.